MW01614695

"I have been counselin heard a story quite like this. At the time the author first confided in me, I told her this blessing had been given for her to share, to give testimony to the providence of God and His redeeming grace. I challenged her to resolve not to hide, but to proclaim this story and to pray for strength and courage to do so. This book is her response."

—REV. DR. MATTHEW MCGOWAN, Retired Parish Associate,
First Presbyterian Church, Gainesville, Georgia

"Everyone needs to hear this story and read this book. During my years as group leader for the *Forgiven and Set Free* study, I have heard many stories—this one is unique. The author testifies to God's power, love, mercy, forgiveness, and redemption in a powerful way and gives Him all of the glory. It is an incredible example of Satan's intent to destroy lives, and of God's power to preserve lives and create beauty out of ashes."

—LYNN HURLEY, Group Leader, *Forgiven and Set Free,*
A Post-Abortion Bible Study for Women, Choices Pregnancy
Care Center, Gainesville, Georgia

"I suggested to my adult Sunday School class that the role of the Church is to point to signs of the Kingdom at work in the midst of a world which has largely forgotten God. This wonderful story does exactly that. It shows us, lovingly and humbly, how the Lord God created an 'unexpected family.' It is a marvelous gift."

—REV. DR. TOM COLLINS, Pastor, Santee Presbyterian Church,
Santee, South Carolina

"I had the pleasure of inviting the author to speak at a Women of Grace monthly luncheon. Her time with us was such a blessing. Our hearts were touched as she humbly shared of a God-ordained reunion with the birth-son she had originally attempted to abort. It was a moving story of how God forgives and redeems through His love. Her book tells the entire story of God's remarkable creation of a new unexpected family."

—SHIRLEY LANGLEY, Women of Grace,First Baptist Church, Elloree, South Carolina

"This is a story of two mothers, a baby, and two families whose lives took a very winding road. It's a painful story about infertility, miscarriages, abortion, and separation. But it is also a joyful story about answered prayers, forgiveness, adoption, reconciliation, hope, and grace. Above all, this is a story, like every truly great story—about salvation."

—PASTOR KEVIN MADDEN, First Baptist Church, Washington, Georgia

Unexpected FAMILY

A LIFE SAVED—A LIFE REDEEMED

Dogwood Blossoms
Emma Moore 2015

Unexpected FAMILY

A LIFE SAVED—A LIFE REDEEMED

BETTE NOBLE

Unexpected Family: A Life Saved—A Live Redeemed

Copyright © 2015 by Bette Noble

ISBN 978-0-578-15925-6

The persons and events portrayed in this work of non-fiction are real. Persons are identified by their actual names only with permission given to the author. All other names are duly noted by footnote to be fictional. Locations and institutions are not specifically described or named.

Unless otherwise noted, verses are taken from the Holy Bible, New International Version®. NIV®. Copyright © 1973, 1978, 1984, 2011, by Biblica, Inc.™ Used by permission

Editor: Gloria Spencer
Cover design: Sean Allen
Interior design and typeset: Katherine Lloyd, The DESK

Library of Congress Control Number: 2015905600

Printed in the United States of America

DEDICATED

to

Jesse and Connie Moore
Parents chosen and blessed by God

For you created my inmost being;
you knit me together in my mother's womb.
I praise you because I am fearfully and wonderfully made;
your works are wonderful,
I know that full well.

My frame was not hidden from you
when I was made in the secret place,
when I was woven together in the depths of the earth.
Your eyes saw my unformed body;
all the days ordained for me were written in your book
before one of them came to be.

(Psalm 139:13-16)

CONTENTS

ACKNOWLEDGMENTS

*T*his story would not exist without Michael Moore, his wife, Denise, and his adoptive parents, Jesse and Connie Moore. Michael had the courage and perseverance to search for his birth-mother not knowing what he might find. He had the fortitude to continue searching despite many dead-ends. His parents as well as his wife supported him in his search and constantly prayed for a successful conclusion. They spent many hours actively involved in the process. Their confidence in their roles as Michael's parents and as his wife was solid and unshakable no matter what was revealed. Thank you, Moore family, for the support you gave to Michael in his search for his birth-mother.

The wise counsel given by Stephi Fisher about meeting my birth-son for the first time undergirded the initial interaction and ongoing relationship with prayer and love.

My longtime friend and prayer partner, Kay Shirer, and our mutual friends, Jerry and Peggy Boggus, challenged me to share the story in media, believing it to be inspirational and a testimony to God's love and salvation. A writing contest connected to an inspirational magazine birthed the idea of the book, the first draft of which I wrote in fifteen days to meet the approaching deadline.

Laura Petherbridge, speaker and author and my friend and former colleague at Crown Financial Ministries, offered a key recommendation—"You need my former critique group to mentor you in writing"—and agreed to introduce me to a wonderful group of ladies: Ruth Trippy, Donna Lott, Hope Welborn, Peggy Moore, and early on, LeAnne Benfield Martin, Laurie Fuller, and editor, Gloria Spencer. They are all accomplished wordsmiths and have become good friends. They gave generously of their time and talent and enabled this technical writer to compose and produce a publishable book about how God changed my life and united my family members.

A number of additional readers suggested additions that expanded the scope of the book and made it richer. Thanks to my freshman roommate and dearest friend, Margie Miller Clark, who also lived through part of the story with me, and to readers Susan Biddy, Lynn Hurley, Susan Nish, Bobbylea Pennington, Chuck Thompson, Kay Stroman, and Peggy Moore.

Chuck Bentley, CEO of Crown, believed in this book and encouraged its publication from his first knowledge of the topic. At the celebration banquet of the 2013 Crown Global Conference, Chuck invited me to tell the story of our *Unexpected Family* and invited Michael to sing one of his original Christian songs.

Grateful appreciation also goes to my former roommate, known in the book as Hannah Smith, who rushed me to the hospital when I was in critical condition and prayed for me and my unborn baby. No one else knew our situation or how desperately we both needed the Lord's intervention to survive.

The support and positive feedback from our pastors, Dr. Jasper Keith and Rev. Paul Evans, our retired parish associate, Dr. Matt McGowan, and our church elders was significant and uplifting. I am grateful for their Christian love, prayers, and acceptance.

Many thanks are due to my beloved sons, Mark and Clark Noble, who opened their hearts and embraced their previously unknown half-brother and his family. Their support and encouragement while writing this book inspired me to continue until it was completed.

And lastly, I give my everlasting gratitude to my husband,

ACKNOWLEDGMENTS

Steve Noble, who loved me and married me forty-three years ago despite prior events, and who has walked with me and advised me throughout this remarkable journey as we have come to know and love this new unexpected branch of our family.

My highest praises go to the Lord for orchestrating the events in 1970 to save Michael's life, and perhaps my life also, and in 2010, for supernaturally bringing beauty out of the ashes, connecting us, redeeming my life, and giving us a great blessing—our *Unexpected Family.*

One

THE VOICE,
THE PRAYER, THE CALL

*M*om!"

The young man's voice sounded urgent.

"What is it, son? Are you in trouble?" I spoke out loud in the dark room as I sat bolt upright in bed. It was a Thursday night in October of 2010.

Where did that voice come from? I wondered. Immediately, the thought came that it might be a prompting to pray for our younger son, Clark, a Marine helicopter pilot on deployment in the Middle East. But it also could have been our older son, Mark, who was in school in another state studying physical therapy.

"Lord, help my son! Lord, please help my son. Lord, please help my son."

On my knees beside the bed, the frantic prayer gushed out over and over. When the prompting began to subside, I glanced at my husband. He was still sound asleep. Exhausted, my face wet with tears, I lay down, and eventually dropped off to sleep.

As soon as I awoke the next morning the voice in the dream came to mind. What was that about? Why had I prayed, "Lord, help my son," instead of using their names? I usually do not dwell on my dreams, but that voice and my response felt unusually vivid. It must have meant something important, but what?

I emailed both sons and each thanked me for praying for him. They had both had problems the previous night, but to my mind, nothing they mentioned seemed worthy of a dramatic summons to prayer in the middle of the night.

⚜

Monday morning I found a cryptic voice message on my office phone. The man said he had something personal to discuss with me. The only information he gave was his name, his workplace, and his office and cell phone numbers. That was not unusual. I worked for a well-known Christian financial ministry and frequently received calls for consultation about finances or career choices. I had a full morning schedule following up on action items from meetings, so it was mid-afternoon before I could return the call.

I entered the phone number. It was routine; just like any call return. But this was to be no ordinary conversation. At that moment, I had no idea how fundamentally my life was about to be turned upside down.

"Mr. Moore, this is Elizabeth[1] Noble returning your call from this morning."

"Mrs. Noble, thank you for calling me back," he said in a very polite voice. "I have a personal matter I would like to discuss with you dating all the way back to 1970."

He paused.

My thoughts swirled. 1970. What could this be about? The voice was obviously a young man. What could he have to discuss with me from forty years ago? Oh, God! 1970!

"I have been trying to locate my birth-mother and your name turned up in my search. I would like to talk with you about that, if you are willing."

---

1 Elizabeth is my given name, Bette is a nickname.

I gasped.

"If you do not want to talk with me, you can choose to hang up now," he added.

I collapsed back into my desk chair. I tried to respond, but I could only manage to stammer something about calling him back after work.

My heart pounding, I slowly returned the phone to its holder. For a long time I sat, dazed, trying to catch my breath, gather my thoughts, and evaluate what had just happened. That call was a possibility I had occasionally considered, but never expected!

In 1970, I was a single graduate student in a PhD. program, working for my major professor on a research assistantship. Through my relationship with an older student at the university, I had become pregnant. After several attempts to obtain an illegal abortion, I found myself months later in an emergency room with severe hemorrhaging. To my great dismay and shock, I learned I was in labor. I was taken to the maternity ward and soon delivered a live baby, about three months premature.

The infant was quickly taken away from my view and rushed to the neonatal department. The next day a social worker came to talk with me about my plans for the baby. Placing the baby for adoption was an option to consider if I could not care for it. She said she would give me time to think about it and would come back the next day. Feeling this was the best option for both the baby and me, I decided while she was still in the room to sign the papers to transfer parental authority to the state Family and Children's Services department.

After spending two days recovering in the hospital, I went right back to my graduate classes. I pushed the matter to the back of my mind and went on with my life plan. I had work to do to keep my mind busy. The following month I would be presenting my research paper at a conference.

Three months later, a social worker called my apartment. She informed me the baby had survived after two months in the hospital, a month in foster care, and had been placed with an adoptive family. It was a closed adoption; common at that time. Birth-mothers had no input in the placement of their babies and received no updates as they do today. As far as I knew, the notification about the adoption was the end of the story. No contact, no information—until that call in October, 2010.

I was stunned by the realization that my prayers for "my son" in the middle of that Thursday night must have been for this other son whom I had seen only at the moment of his birth. I learned later he had been searching almost three years for his birth-mother. Earlier that week he had cried out to God for a breakthrough. The night after my prayers he had put together clues from the limited information he had about his birth-mother in a new way and found a match on an online university alumni directory—leading to me.

At some point in the years since his birth, when he came to mind and I wondered how he was doing or if he was even alive, I had begun to pray for him. Around the time of his birth date in April that year I realized this would be a landmark birthday—his fortieth. It occurred to me if he ever considered locating his birth-mother, this might be the time.

Now the impossible had happened. There were so many things to think about. Number one in my mind was telling my husband, Steve. Thankfully, before our marriage I had told him about the adopted baby. But I wanted to find someone else, a counselor or consultant, who could give me some perspective on how to deal with this bombshell.

The afternoon I had received that earthshaking phone call, still in shock, I had to keep a physical therapy appointment. Sitting in the waiting room, I absently flipped through pages of a magazine. An ad for a book by Jamie Lee Curtis caught my eye.

"Tell me again about the night I was born. Tell me again how you would adopt me and be my parents... Tell me again about the first time you held me in your arms."[2]

This book was new to me, and just reading about it softened my heart. It reminded me this was not all about me, but about the son I had never known. Through God's grace, I had been offered the opportunity to meet him—his search had located me and contact had been made.

My mind elsewhere, I went through the motions of the exercises, talked with the therapist, left the office, and walked out to the parking lot. Where were my keys? After some digging, I finally located them at the bottom of my purse. Thank goodness for the remote entry button.

I slid into the driver's seat, but my hands were shaking so it was hard to get the key into the ignition. With my head still spinning, I realized talking to Michael Moore that evening would be out of the question. I needed more time to process all this. I decided I would call and leave a short message to let him know I would get in touch later in the week.

On the drive home, I tried to determine what I should do. Could I just pretend—even to myself—that none of this had happened? Could I now, after all these years, acknowledge this

---

2 Curtis, Jamie Lee, *Tell Me Again about the Night I Was Born*. New York, NY: Harpercollins Childrens Books, 1996.

son to my family and friends? What would they think of me? What did God think of me?

After only a few minutes, I realized I was following my familiar life pattern: trying to figure it all out on my own. But I could not. Who in the world could help me deal with all this? Was there anyone I knew who had experienced anything similar?

The place to begin, I knew, was to consult the one Person who already knew all about it. I had been a Christian most of my life, but still found it difficult to depend on God or others. I prayed: *Lord, please help me know what to do. I always wondered if this would happen one day, but this is much more than I can handle by myself. The reality of this man contacting me is overwhelming. I never imagined it might feel like this! Please come along beside me, guide my thoughts and lead me to godly people who can help and advise me. On one hand, I am filled with joy and amazement, but on the other, I am terrified of exposure and all the negative possibilities.*

Steve will help me—I interrupted my conversation with God—He's always good at thinking through options. I caught myself and returned to my prayer.

*Calm my fear, Lord, and help me focus on **Your** wisdom and guidance. Even with all these mixed emotions, I thank you, Lord, for the phone call. Guide me and be with me on the road ahead.*

I drove up the driveway, put the car in park, and turned off the motor.

Thank you, Lord. Thank you. In Jesus' precious name, Amen.

Two

CONNECTING

*S*teve!"

Still out of breath, I barged into his study and closed the door. He stopped what he was doing and waited for me to continue.

"I had an unusual message on my phone at work today."

Sensing my anxiety, he silently waited for me to explain.

"It was a man who said he had a personal matter to discuss with me." Tears welled in my eyes. "I called him back, and—" I paused, searching for words. "—and it was the baby; you know, the one I told you about. The baby I placed for adoption." My husband's eyes grew wide. "Really? Are you sure?"

"Yes, I'm positive." Tears were flowing now. "I'm sure it's him."

Steve cleared his throat. "Frankly, I'm surprised it took him this long to contact you. I'd have thought this would have happened years ago. Did you confirm anything with him?"

"No. I told him I couldn't talk right then and I would call back after work. But I'm not ready to talk to him tonight."

"You're sure it's him? And if it is, do you even want to admit you are his mother?"

"I don't know. It—it's such a shock." Feeling too shaky to stand, I slid into a chair.

"I would be very careful and check him out before you admit anything. You don't know what he's after. He might try to blackmail you or something. There are all sorts of bad situations with these kinds of connections."

"I know, and that scares me. I could tell he was a little nervous, but there was something so genuine in his voice, so respectful and sincere. I felt in my heart I could trust him."

"Well, this has been a long time coming." Steve pulled me to my feet, then hugged me. Holding me close, he added, "We'll pray about it and ask for guidance."

That night at bedtime we prayed together for wisdom about whom to call—someone who might have experience with such an unusual situation. I awoke the next morning with a friend in mind I had known from ministry. Her Christmas letter a few years earlier had described meeting her oldest granddaughter who had been born to her then-high-school-aged daughter and placed for adoption. The granddaughter had decided in her twenties to contact her birth family.

I had not seen this friend in several years, but I thought she might be able to give me some needed perspective. Though she lived several states away, my stomach twisted at the thought of revealing my situation to anyone. I was not ready to have my circumstances become public, so I determined I would tell her I was seeking advice for a friend.

I was working from home that day and had the house to myself. I laid out a legal pad on my desk to take notes and placed the call. After some small talk and catching up on each other's families, I said, "Stephi, the reason I called is really unusual. I have a very good friend who received a call out of the blue similar to your contact with your granddaughter. This just happened and my friend is at a loss how to proceed. She's had no contact and no information since the baby's birth."

"You say she has never met or talked with this person?"

"No, just the unexpected call from a man she believes is her birth child. She told him she would have to call back."

"That's a little different than our situation," she said. She told me her granddaughter had just wanted historical information about her birth family. Stephi had been the one who took the initiative to meet her in person. She arranged for them to meet at a neutral location—a restaurant.

I asked Stephi what she thought would be helpful for my friend to know.

"Tell her to pray for wisdom on how to build a relationship with her newfound offspring," Stephi advised. "And pray to be open and vulnerable. When I met my new granddaughter for the first time I felt it was very important to tell her that whenever God had brought her to my mind, I had prayed for her and that I was so glad for the chance to meet her."

With tears, fears and laughter, the restaurant meeting had been such an amazing time of getting to know one another, she said. And her granddaughter had turned out to be a wonderful young woman.

"God needs to be in it," Stephi added. "Leave everything in the birth child's court. Let it be however he wants it to be. Adopted kids want to know about their history. Think about when you meet someone for the first time how wonderful it can be. It's the normal thing for you to want to get to know them."

"So you think my friend needs to respond and connect?'

"Absolutely. Oh, and one more thing. If your friend has children, it is very important they be told about this new half-sibling."

Oh, dear God, help me!

I almost said it out loud. I had not thought about telling our sons. Panic gripped me.

Reining in my thoughts, I realized Stephi was still talking. She said she had shared her wonderful story of reconciliation with several women's groups.

My panic intensified. *What if God wants me to share my story with others?* The thought of exposing my situation publicly terrified me even more than the prospect of having to tell our sons.

I pulled myself together enough to thank Stephi and tell her I would pass her advice to my friend. At her request, I said I would let her know how it went.

I was relieved when the conversation was over and I could confront my fears. I bowed my head. *Thank you, God, for answering our prayers from last night. Stephi was exactly the right person to talk with. How wonderful to know someone I trust has been in a similar situation and survived. I think now I am ready to talk to Michael Moore.* I asked the Lord to calm my spirit and give me the right words to say.

⁕

That evening I returned Mr. Moore's call.

"Mrs. Noble, thank you so much for calling me back," he said politely, with a distinctly Southern accent. "I was hoping you would."

After exchanging pleasantries, I asked him to tell me about himself. He gave his birth date, the city, and the hospital.

"So you were born in the city hospital," I repeated, not knowing what else to say.

"Yes, I was," he said. "I was a preemie, born at six months, and spent about two months in the neonatal unit after my birth."

My breath caught, but I continued, "When were you adopted?"

"I was three months old."

Oh my goodness, I thought. That was exactly when the social worker had called to tell me the baby had been adopted. I remembered that call well. I had been so relieved to hear the adoption had been completed.

"The couple who adopted me had experienced nine miscarriages in nine years. I had some birth-related issues with mild cerebral palsy and wore braces on my legs for a while, but I'm okay now and was even able to play all the sports growing up."

I was not surprised to hear of his birth-related issues. Years earlier I had been involved in testing severely handicapped children. Many of them had histories of birth trauma similar to his, and many were premature. In fact, under the circumstances, I thought it a miracle Michael's problems had not been more severe.

"Where did you go to school?" I asked.

"I went to a private academy in our town. I was a good student and earned a scholarship to go to a small private college for two years until my sister—two years younger and also adopted—started college, and then I transferred to a public university. I was a computer science major. It took me six years to finish because I was in a work-study program with a telecommunications company. Now I work with the statewide university IT system as a database engineer and programmer."

Another miracle, I thought. He hadn't been harmed mentally. He was obviously bright. He liked data and analysis, a lot like me. Amazing!

"And your family?"

"I am married to a great woman who is a nurse. We have three children—eight-year-old twins, a boy and a girl, and a four-year-old son."

I smiled at that statement. My dad and his sister were twins.

Then my heart skipped a beat. Wait a minute. Those were not just any children he was talking about. Those were my grandchildren!

I took a deep breath. Almost as if hearing the words without willing to speak them, I said, "I am your birth-mother." I could not hold it in any longer. The information he gave had confirmed it. His description exactly matched the location and circumstances of the birth of the baby I had borne in 1970.

"I'm so glad to finally talk to you," he said. "I hope to meet you some day."

Wait! Let's slow down here, I thought. *I just found out about you. I'm not sure I'm ready to think about meeting you face-to-face.*

"I'm glad to talk to you, too," I said. "It was quite a surprise to me to hear from you. It's good to know you are doing well and have a family. I don't know quite how to respond at this point. I need some time to process all this. But we'll talk again."

"All right," he said. "I look forward to it."

After we said good-bye I sat still for a long time with my head spinning.

Did this really happen? Am I awake? Yes! I shook myself back to consciousness. *This is real! I now know this son I bore forty years ago, under difficult circumstances and against all odds, is alive and thriving despite the circumstances of his birth and all I tried to do to prevent him from coming into the world. He is married and has three children and I just talked to him!*

Sweet Jesus, how did you arrange this? Dear Lord, this is truly amazing. What a blessing to know he is alive and whole.

Three

REUNION

*H*e's the one!"

Steve looked up from his desk and smiled at my obvious excitement as I made my announcement. "So you called him back. What do you think? Sit down and tell me what you found out."

"He confirmed all his birth details." I continued to talk as I settled into a chair. "And he's married to a nurse and has three children. The older two are twins, eight years old, boy and girl, just like Dad and Aunt Frances. The younger boy is four."

"What about his physical condition?" Steve asked when I stopped for a breath. "Three months premature is really early."

"That's the really good news. After all I put him through, he had only mild cerebral palsy, wore braces for a while, but was able to play sports in school." I paused in case Steve wanted to comment. But when he didn't, I continued, "He's quite bright. He graduated from the state university in computer science and did work-study with a telecommunications company. He's a database engineer and programmer with the statewide university IT department." I smiled at our similar interests. "Isn't that amazing? He likes data and analysis like me."

"Sounds like you covered a lot in one phone call. What are you going to do now?"

"He mentioned he would like to meet me someday. I need to think about that. It's doable; they live only an hour south of the university." I stopped for a moment and sighed as all the negative possibilities flooded my thoughts. "I'd like to meet him, but I'm afraid of other people finding out. I'm so ashamed of having a baby out of wedlock. I haven't even mentioned it to any of my doctors—never put the real number of births on my medical history. And what about Mark and Clark? How do I tell them?"

"There's a lot to think about, but if you do decide to meet him, I'm definitely going with you. You're not doing this alone."

"Believe me, I wouldn't go without you. I'll need your support. This is scary to even think about."

My curiosity soon overcame my fear. Two days later, after more discussions with Steve, I called my new-found son, Michael, and asked if we and our spouses could meet the following Saturday. We agreed on a time and a place about an hour away, halfway between our homes.

That week, during a call to my best friend Kay, I asked her to pray for me at the appointed time without telling her why. She graciously agreed, no questions asked.

When Saturday came I was very anxious. As Steve and I drove to the meeting place, questions kept rolling around in my head. *What will it be like? What will he look like? What will we say? How does a person greet a child as an adult whom they've never met before?*

Once we arrived, I began to open the car door, then stopped. "Steve, let's pray for the Holy Spirit's presence to be with us and help me calm down. I'm almost shaking."

Steve held my hand while I prayed. "Dear Lord, this is such a miracle for this son to be alive and able to meet with us. I'm so nervous. I pray you will calm my heart." I took a deep breath. "Lord, I don't know what to expect. Please be with us and help us to respond to each other with love."

Steve kissed me and squeezed my hand. Then he came around the car to open the door and help me stand. Feeling more composed and at peace after our prayer, I smiled at Steve, grasped his hand very tightly, and we walked into the restaurant.

I needn't have wondered about how to greet Michael. An excited-looking man ran up to me and said, "I'd like to hug you, if that's okay."

Of course it was. From that moment, I felt swept along by the current of his energy. None of my earlier fears held sway. After our hug we introduced our spouses and moved toward a table in a large, mostly empty, side room.

I was struck by how different Michael looked from my expectations. To my surprise, he didn't closely resemble either of my sons or even his birth-father, which is what I had envisioned. Instead, to my amazement, he looked a lot like my dad, with a high forehead and broad smile, but with my big blue eyes.

His slight limp caused me to shudder. It was undoubtedly the result of his premature birth and mild cerebral palsy. Seeing the impact of my attempted late-term abortion on his body was difficult, but I knew the damage could have been worse—so much worse. I thanked the Lord for protecting him.

After we were seated, we all seemed to be a little nervous and unsure how the meeting would proceed.

"I've been looking forward to this all day!" I said, hoping to break the ice.

"Can I get anyone something to drink or eat?" Steve offered. Something to drink was fine for me and also for Michael and

Denise. Steve went to order coffee for us and sweet tea and Coke for them. Meanwhile, Michael laid out pictures he had brought.

There he was as a newly-adopted baby, still tiny and frail, just five and a half pounds at three months old. Later pictures showed him as a handsome, healthy little boy and young man. His parents were a nice-looking couple and seemed very pleasant, as did his younger sister, Jennifer, also adopted. Michael said his father was a retired teacher and state patrolman, currently a farmer, cattleman, and sawmill owner/operator; his mother was a retired kindergarten teacher and part-time beautician, currently doing catering and event coordination (wedding receptions, anniversaries, birthdays, etc.) with a group of friends.

Pictures of his children intrigued me. Baby and toddler pictures of the twins, and more recent pictures of the younger son, brought tears to my eyes. Evan and Emma, the twins, and Aaron, the baby of the family, were indeed beautiful children.

This introduction to his life was difficult to process and translate into reality. These were the pictures of a stranger, but they were also pictures of my child, my first-born, and his family. The children were my grandchildren. What an amazing experience!

I put pictures of our family on the table to pass around, some recent and some older.

"So I have two brothers?" Michael broke into a broad grin as he scanned the pictures. "I've always wanted a brother. Do they live nearby? Are they married?"

"Our older son, Mark, is thirty-five. He's been living in South Carolina for thirteen years and is now in physical therapy school. Clark, our younger son, is twenty-eight, an officer and helicopter pilot in the U.S. Marine Corps. He is currently on deployment, based on a small Navy carrier in the Indian Ocean.

He will complete his deployment in December when the ship arrives at home port in San Diego where he's based. He'll be home in time for Christmas. Neither one is married."

"Wow! A pilot and a physical therapist. I can't wait to meet them."

"We'll have to take it one step at a time," I cautioned. "I never told anyone about you, including my parents, so our sons know nothing. It will be December before we'll see them both at the same time. I'll wait till we're all together to tell them they have a newly-discovered half-brother. And then it will be up to them."

"We'll have to pray really hard about that," Michael responded.

Michael told us he, his wife, and his adoptive parents had been praying for about three years that he would find his birth-mother, and if she was not a Christian, to have an opportunity to share Jesus with her. He said his parents were very supportive of our meeting and were praying as we met, asking for God's blessing on our time together.

I cannot explain it, but I felt at ease and somehow already bonded with the man sitting beside me, this man I had brought into the world forty years earlier.

We talked for a while as a foursome, he and I, Steve and Denise, just getting acquainted and hearing about their children.

"Michael, I have a big question about how you found me. Were you working on your search a week ago Friday?"

"Yes, I worked on the search last Thursday and Friday evenings. It wasn't until late Friday night that I found your name and contact information in the University's online alumni directory. Why do you ask?"

"I had a strange dream and that led me to pray for help for my son on Thursday night, but I didn't name the son. I wonder if it had something to do with what you found. Were you sure you had found the right person on Friday night?"

"Of course, I wasn't completely sure, but I felt all the pieces fit together like never before. I had always known I was adopted and there was someone out there I was related to, but when I was younger, I didn't want to start a search and maybe hurt my parents in any way. I was also cautious about finding out something I did not want to know. I didn't want to be hurt by learning my birth-mother wanted nothing to do with me."

"I can understand that. I'm sure many birth-mothers are conflicted about connecting with their birth child who might call and want to meet. I've had mixed feelings myself, Steve can tell you that. But we've prayed for guidance and I felt we should arrange a meeting." I paused for a moment, hoping he was okay with what I just said. "Back to your search, have you been searching a long time? And why did you start to search?"

"As I grew older, into my thirties, I reached a point where I needed to know. About three years ago I started my search. Although the state's adoption reunion registry provided search services, I decided the non-identifying information I obtained from the registry and the details given by my parents were enough to conduct the search myself. I knew your home town and that you were a psychology major at the state university and in *Who's Who*. I told myself, 'I can find this lady.' Denise and my attorney called and emailed people who might know someone who could be helpful, such as the dean of women. We also went to the library and looked through the university yearbooks and the *Who's Who* books for that time period.

"During that time I identified seven or eight women. You were not the first woman I called. But this time I sensed I had the right one."

"What was different this time?"

"Early in the search, our county superior court judge reviewed my records after I asked if he could help me in any way. After waiting a few weeks and wondering if I would hear back, he called. Very briefly, he said, 'Here's all I can give you—"Baby Boy Jones." Good luck.' Thinking the name was an alias, I put that information aside. But recently, after all the dead ends over the last three years, I remembered the clue and thought it was worth a search. I decided to look for a woman with that last name."

True, Jones is a commonly-used alias, but it happened to be my maiden name. Michael had no way of knowing that, however.

"What else was different?" I continued.

"The other important difference was, on Monday of that week, I had prayed with an increased desperation. On my knees, with my head on the floor, I was begging God for a breakthrough to find my birth-mother, and maybe through her, my birth-father. I don't know why I felt so burdened and so urgent, but I felt I just had to find you, and soon. I prayed, 'God, please open the door to let me find her and maybe my birth-father also. I pray they are both okay. I just hope it isn't too late.'"

I looked at Michael in amazement. "So that same week, on Thursday night, I had that dream of my son calling, 'Mom!' I woke up and desperately pleaded for the Lord to 'help my son,' not knowing which son it was, never thinking it might be you. And the following night you put all the pieces together. It was then you found a woman whose last name was Jones in the online directory that matched all the non-identifying information sent to you from social services and the details given to your parents."

"Yes, exactly. I waited all weekend and then called your office early Monday morning. It looks like God certainly answered our prayers!"

There we sat together, eight days later, silently considering God's wondrous ways. We were all stunned at the thought that

God had not only heard Michael's prayer, but had also enlisted me to pray, unknowingly requesting help for my birth-son.

Lord God, you truly heed the earnest prayers of your people.

At that point I asked if our spouses would let us have some time alone. There was more I needed to share with Michael that might cause him to turn his back and walk away. Steve and Denise graciously stood and moved away together.

After they left, Michael said, "The first thing I meant to say to you is, thank you for bringing me into the world. I am so glad to be alive. God was good to me, placing me with Momma and Daddy. They have given me a wonderful home and have been great parents. I'm also grateful for my wife and marriage and my beautiful children. At one point I was afraid we might have to adopt. I was desperate to have offspring of my own so I would have someone I was really related to."

I knew I could not take credit for bringing him into the world. I swallowed hard and pressed on to the subject that was making my heart feel heavy.

"Michael, maybe I should not tell you this, but I feel I need to be honest with you. The reason you were premature was I had attempted a late-term abortion."

I braced myself for his response.

"But, thankfully, by the grace of God, you survived."

Michael looked into my eyes. "It does not matter," he said. "It's okay. I knew that trying to find you might reveal some things I really did not want to know. I have been prepared for that. The non-identifying information from the state adoption reunion registry was compiled by a social worker. She mentioned an abortion attempt in her summary notes. That was probably more than she should have included in her report, but I'm glad I had that information in advance. So I knew a little bit about that already. But it just does not matter."

He put his hand on mine. "God has forgiven and redeemed all that," he continued gently, "and you shouldn't worry about it anymore. The important thing is I'm alive and healthy. I've had a good life and I'm just so glad to finally meet you."

"I'm so glad to meet you, too," I squeaked, choking back tears. "This has been an amazing time, to say the least." I felt my emotions reaching the limit of my control and I was beginning to tremble inside. "But, it's about time for us to go," I said abruptly. "I wonder if Steve and Denise are in the restaurant." We found them in the main section at a table, apparently having a good conversation.

We gave our final hugs. Just before we left, Michael invited us to come to his church in three weeks to hear him sing a solo with the choir, a Chris Tomlin song, "I Will Rise." Directed by his wife, the children of the church—including his own—would be interpreting the words using sign language. I told him I would have to let him know.

The truth is, I was still very afraid of being recognized. I was not at all comfortable being with Michael in his church where he was well-known. Several people there were aware he had found his birth-mother. I had only known about him less than a week and needed time to process this new reality in my life.

I had such conflicting feelings. On the positive side, I was extremely grateful to meet Michael and to find his parents were devout Christians and he was also a person of strong faith. It was especially important to me that he was alive and healthy with a successful career, a solid marriage, and a lovely family. On the negative side, I was not ready to publicly embrace this new relationship and openly reveal the evidence of my immoral past. Steve and I had agreed it was even more imperative in today's world of social networking to delay any public disclosure until our sons and our pastor had been informed.

We said good-bye and I made it to the car before I broke down in tears. I was overwhelmed with emotion. What a profound life experience; what a blessing to meet this fine man, my own flesh and blood, and his lovely wife as well! In spite of my fears and reservations, I was so glad God had orchestrated our meeting this side of heaven.

Thank you, Lord.

Four

OBEDIENCE

*A*t the time I received the life-changing call from Michael, I had been participating at my workplace in Henry and Richard Blackaby's *Experiencing God* Bible study.[3] We were assigned daily readings. But the week prior to Michael's Sunday choir special, I had read nothing. The middle of the night prior to the weekly meeting found me cramming through the lessons and writing the responses for the next day's topic, "Adjusting Your Life to God."

In class the next day, I opened my book. My eyes fell on a question that stunned me.

"What was the most meaningful statement or Scripture you read today?"

My written response? *"Obedience requires adjustment."*

"Reword the statement or Scripture into a prayer of response to God."

"Lord, I want to be obedient; help me to do what You want me to do."

---

3 Blackaby, H., Blackaby R., and King, C. *Experiencing God –Member Book.* Nashville, TN: LifeWay Press, 2009.

"What does God want you to do in response to today's study?"

"Go to Michael's church on Sunday."

I blinked and looked again. How did those words get on the page? I honestly did not remember writing them. But there before me in the book was the instruction spelled out in black and white and in my own script. I glanced upward and said inwardly, *Okay, God. That was clear!* I wanted to shout out loud to the group, *You would not believe what I just read on this page!* But I did not say it. I was not ready to go public. So I contained myself for the remainder of the study session and mused about this not-so-subtle way God was using to communicate.

After work, I drove home still shaking my head over what appeared to be another direct communication from God. With the *Experiencing God* workbook in hand, I walked into Steve's study and placed the open book in front of him.

"Read this." I pointed to the handwritten response. "Can you believe I wrote this last night? I was up in the wee hours catching up on my reading for the meeting. I don't remember it at all."

"You're kidding. Are you sure you were awake?"

"I have no explanation. At lunch today, when I opened the book for the group study, the words were there." I picked up the book and held it close. "It's like God is saying I'm being too skittish about going to Michael's church Sunday. What do you think?"

"I think we can avoid an open connection and be discreet," Steve offered. "This contact with Michael is all new and I agree you need to be careful in public, at least until Mark and Clark know about it."

"It would be great to hear him sing. When we were in the restaurant he didn't mention singing in the choir, so when he asked as we were leaving, it caught me off-guard. We've talked on the phone several times since, and he's asked if we are coming." I sat down, deep in thought. "What about this? No conversation at church, then meet elsewhere after the service so we won't call attention to any relationship between us."

"Good thought. Somewhere on the edge of town," Steve added.

"So it's a plan! I'll get in touch with Michael." I reached for my cellphone.

I told Michael we would be coming on Sunday and explained our wishes. He was very excited and invited us to have dinner at their house to meet the children. We agreed to connect after church at the Golden Pantry convenience store on the edge of town. From there we would follow him to his home.

The church was a magnificent old brick structure with a beautiful sanctuary and historic stained-glass windows. We sat near the back. Since we were strangers, a number of people around us introduced themselves, interested in our reason for being there. "Just visiting in the area," we told them.

"Look, there's Denise," Steve whispered and nodded toward the front. Denise was walking up the aisle and looking around. She spotted us and smiled. No doubt she found Michael and told him our seating location. When the choir filed into the sanctuary from the rear, he looked back to where we were sitting. His face lit up with the most vibrant smile. This was only the second time I had seen him and I could not take my eyes off him.

The preliminaries and the sermon seemed to last forever. *Would the choir ever start singing?* Finally, they stood, and Michael moved to the side apart from the rest. The children stepped onto the platform, took their positions, and the music began.

The performance was wonderful! Michael sang beautifully. It was so special to see him in that role. The choir and organ were excellent and the children were very good signing the words. I tried to pick out Michael's children. Of course, that was difficult from our back row view. I could see a little girl that looked like one I remembered from the pictures. If only we were closer to the front—

After the service, we drove to the Golden Pantry and waited for Michael. Denise and the children had gone home separately. Michael arrived and jumped out of his truck, a big grin on his face as he gave me my third hug. "Hi, Mama B. It's great to see you again!" That was the name he had given me during a phone call that week. He shook Steve's hand vigorously. "Good to see you again, Mr. Steve."

"Good to see you too, Michael. It's been hard keeping Bette under control but I was able to keep her quiet during the service. She's very excited."

"Michael, I'm so glad we came," I said, ignoring Steve's teasing. "Your solo, the choir, and the children's signing were just wonderful! You have a great voice," I added. "We enjoyed the entire service and loved your church."

Michael glanced at his watch. "We can talk more later. It takes a few minutes to get to the house from here. Denise and the kids will be waiting for us." We followed him several miles into the countryside.

At their house we met the three children—eight-year old twins Evan and Emma and four-year-old Aaron. We stooped down to shake hands with each of them since they were a little too shy at first for hugs. Steve had asked Michael ahead of time about their candy favorites so he offered Emma and Aaron Jolly

Ranchers and gave Evan Whoppers. The treats definitely helped break the ice.

The boys were both very blond with straight hair. Emma's was brown and curly. All three had big, blue eyes and were so good-looking! We were introduced as Ms. Bette and Mr. Steve, but as we were told later, Evan whispered to his father, "Is this your birth-mother?" Michael had told them he had found his birth-mother, and it didn't take long for the twins to guess who was there for Sunday dinner. Emma told Michael's mother the next day she had met her "biological" grandmother.

The twins were bright, articulate, and personable. They "showed off" by bringing out all their toys and gadgets to impress us. Each twin had an electronic device they could use to send pictures or messages to each other. Sitting between them and observing this digital interaction was fascinating. Evan seemed very knowledgeable and shared unusual scientific facts from a magazine similar to a *Weekly Reader*. Emma was expressive and very much in charge. She corrected her twin and interpreted for her younger brother who was adorable and talkative but difficult to understand.

It was special to be in their home, a small but very comfortable house on six acres purchased from Michael's parents who lived nearby. Michael and Denise told us they had plans to build onto the house soon. Pictures on the walls filled in the years we had missed—their wedding and the children as babies, toddlers, and students in school.

Tears came to my eyes as I scanned the images, and remorse filled my heart. *Lord, we have lost so many years, but how could we have known? Help us to build relationships with them and be a meaningful part of their lives, especially the children.* Immediately the Lord's promise in Joel 2:25 came to mind: "I will repay you for the years the locusts have eaten."

Thank you, Lord, for bringing us here.

When it was time to eat, we held hands for the blessing. It was such a unique and meaningful experience just to sit at the table together as family members. The children were excited— up and down like popcorn—and after eating Denise's delicious meal, were sent outside to play. Emma's cute play dress and matching pink boots made me chuckle. In their excitement to go out, the boys forgot they were still in church clothes. Denise called them back in to change. Steve and I smiled knowingly at one another. Typical little boys. We remembered those days.

When the children finally closed the door Michael took out his twelve-string guitar and sang, "I've looked for you all my life," a song he had written for Denise and sung to her at their wedding. Although it was written especially for Denise, Michael told me later the words also fit his search for his birth-mother and he wanted to sing it for me, too. We were treated to a concert of two more songs out of more than thirty he had written over the years.

"Bravo!" Steve and I clapped our appreciation.

Michael's voice, accompanied by his excellent guitar playing, was every bit as clear and strong as his solo at church. The lyrics and melodies were quite well done. Most of the compositions had a Christian theme. A sample recording had been produced in hopes of landing a contract someday. Michael promised to send a couple of mp3 files of his favorites.

By the Providence of God, this talented man was my son and these three beautiful young ones were my own grandchildren. And to think they would not exist if my plans for abortion had been successful. The thought seared my heart.

Five

WHITE DOGWOODS

$\mathcal{M}$y mind went back to June, 1969. With all my worldly belongings piled around me in my father's big sedan, borrowed for my move from college to graduate school, I left my parent's home and turned toward the next chapter of my life. Just two weeks before this departure, on the first of June, I had received my undergraduate diploma with my parents and my brother standing proudly as my name was announced, a school tradition for families when each graduate crossed the stage.

A part of me hated to say goodbye to the school. As a high school freshman, I had fallen in love with the church-related college when my church youth group attended a week-long summer camp on the campus. My parents had sacrificed greatly to send me to the college of my choice. Even with a scholarship and work grant, the expense had been much more than anticipated.

It had always been my parents' dream for their children to be college graduates. Because of the Great Depression, neither of them had been able to go far beyond high school. My college career had been a good one. I had done well academically, similar to my high school career when I had placed ninth in my class of over a thousand students. Among other college honors, I was one of only three senior women in my class selected for inclusion in both *Who's Who in American Colleges and Universities* and Mortar Board, a national honor society recognizing college seniors for exemplary scholarship, leadership and service.

I was on my way to the next level in my education, a graduate program at a large public university seven hundred miles away. Though grateful for a fresh start, I also carried a body weakened by mononucleosis and a heart broken by a failed romance.

✤

As I drove, the events of the final semester of my senior year filled my thoughts. Midway through February, 1969, my steady boyfriend, John, had called and asked me to go for a walk. He was handsome, a student senator for the senior class, and a pre-law major. I had admired him since freshman year when we went to a concert together, but we did not date again until our senior year.

I hurried to get ready to meet John at the start of the walking path—it had been a couple of weeks since I had heard from him. He had been off campus for several trips to law school interviews during the six-week winter term. It was a beautiful sunny day as we walked to a grove of trees. He stopped and turned toward me, looked at the ground, cleared his throat, and looked up, but not directly at me.

"Bette, I've been thinking a lot lately and I think it would be best if we stopped dating for a while."

"What do you mean, not see each other for a while?" I stammered, shocked at his words.

"Well, I'm not sure I should be dating right now. I need to concentrate on my grades this semester. It'll make a difference in my standing in my law class."

I felt my eyes getting moist. "John, I don't understand why this is necessary. We had such a good time over Christmas. I thought you liked being with me." His words cut me to the core.

"That's just it—I can't afford to be distracted. I've got my senior thesis to write and I just started my senior survey class plus another required course for my major. I have to ace all of them to make sure my grade point average is as high as possible. The final GPA affects my law class standing and the amount of my financial aid award."

"Okay, that makes a little bit of sense. But it just sounds so drastic not to see each other at all." I took a deep breath. "I guess that means I should return your pin. If we're not dating, I shouldn't be wearing it." I removed his fraternity pin and handed it to him. I was deeply in love with him, but the look on his face told me this was not a temporary separation, and that protesting would make no difference.

In the fall, I had met his parents when they came to campus and took us to dinner. He met my parents when he visited our home during Christmas break. Both parent meetings had gone well from my perspective and I envisioned a wedding in our future. But something had changed. Aside from studies, I suspected someone else had taken my place over the past few weeks. We walked back to the dorm in silence. Determined to keep my composure, I said good-bye, opened the door and ran up the stairs to my room. I buried my face in my pillow and cried until I could cry no more.

This unexpected change called for cancelling my plans for teaching math in the city where John was to attend law school. I took the advice of my psychology professor and responded to an announcement for a new doctoral program in applied psychology at a major university in another state. It required a strong background in both math and psychology, a perfect match for my math major and psychology minor. I completed the application materials as soon as they arrived by mail, sent them back, and waited for a response.

✧

"Hello." I was in the dorm room by myself when I answered the phone. It was the 15th of March, 1969. This one call would change the direction of my life. It was Dr. Douglas Browning[4], the director of the applied psychology program to which I had applied for admission.

"Hello, Dr. Browning! I'm surprised to be talking to you, but very pleased you called instead of mailing a letter."

"Elizabeth, I have reviewed your application and test scores with interest. How would you like to come and join our program as a doctoral student and work on our large federal research grant? You appear to be the kind of student we are looking for. Currently we are in the process of building our program and recruiting high caliber students with excellent mathematical skills and knowledge of psychology." He paused for a moment.

I regained my composure enough to answer, "Thank you for your kind words. I'm grateful my professor gave me your announcement. I didn't know a program like yours existed. It sounds very interesting."

"We would like you to come to our campus early next month and meet with our admissions committee for a formal interview. We'll see if the program is a good fit for you and if you are a good fit for our student class. If all looks good, we will be able to include a generous research stipend as part of the package. For most students the amount should be enough to cover tuition and living expenses. How does that sound?"

Stunned at what he was saying, I sat down with a gasp. "Dr. Browning, all you have told me sounds wonderful. I'll definitely plan to come for an interview. When will that be?" We chatted

---

4 Douglas Browning is an alias, not the program director's real name.

about the time and place then concluded the call. A letter would follow to confirm the invitation.

I was overwhelmed with this surprise offer and grateful the new venture would not require more financial assistance from my parents or other sources. Anticipating a successful interview, I determined to leave the memory of my heartbreak behind, make the most of this exceptional opportunity, and honor my parents' love and support. I didn't know, however, that the coming year would bring one of the most devastating ordeals of my life.

As scheduled, I arrived at the university for my interview with Dr. Browning and the admission committee in early April 1969. Spring was in full bloom and the beauty of the white dogwoods took my breath away. All over the campus of my future academic home the dogwood trees were covered with blossoms. Beautifully landscaped lawns and flower beds showcased them in every open space among the red brick Georgian buildings. Following the student guide during the campus tour along the flower-lined walkways, I soaked in the beauty as I joyfully anticipated being a graduate student at this fine university.

Meeting my major professor, Dr. Browning, was pleasant—like greeting a favorite uncle. The admissions committee was cordial and the interview very positive. An official acceptance would come in the mail. Dr. Browning and I talked at length about the program he had invited me to join. I met some of the other students and professors, and toured the Psychology Building. I felt welcomed and excited about this wonderful opportunity and looked forward to working with this outstanding man, affectionately known to his students as "Doc."

In spite of the good interview and the lovely surroundings, I was frustrated I had not found a place to live when I returned in two and a half months to begin the summer semester. Fortunately, just before leaving the Psychology Building, I met two female students in the lobby. We talked for a while and had a good conversation. I asked where they were living and if they had any suggestions for my lodging, starting in the summer. One of the girls, Sharon, was just entering graduate school and was moving into an apartment in June. She graciously offered to share her one-bedroom apartment with me through the end of the fall term or until I made other arrangements.

Brightened and encouraged by my interview at the university, I returned to my small college campus for the final two months of my undergraduate career. Graduation was coming, almost overshadowed in our dorm by the excitement of a couple of engaged friends anticipating their June marriages. Their joy only served to remind me of my romantic breakup earlier that spring.

At the time, I did not have a strong personal relationship with the Lord to guide and nurture me through the heartbreak that again welled up inside me. I was a "good" person, raised in the church. I had accepted Christ at age nine and been baptized. Through my teens I had been extremely active in our church's high school youth group and choir. Initially, I had been involved in the college student ministry. But I had not developed the firm spiritual foundation needed to weather this major storm in my life.

Determined to set aside past disappointment, I set my face again toward the future. As my cloud began to lift, another setback occurred—I became quite ill and was diagnosed with mononucleosis complicated by strep throat. A local doctor treated me and put me on the road to recovery. Although weak and low on energy, I pushed myself to make up classes, completed the three courses required to enter the PhD graduate program, and graduated with my class.

After a short visit at home with my family and the long drive to my new location, I arrived in the large university town in mid-June, just in time for the summer semester. I moved in with Sharon and shared her apartment through the summer and fall.

Recovery from my illness slowed my return to full energy. Although I had planned to begin classes during the summer, there was ample work to be done with the research program. Dr. Browning agreed for me to work full time for the program over the summer and wait to begin classes in the fall. I enjoyed the temporary change from the challenging honors courses of my undergraduate years. This gave me extra time to study and learn about the large-scale project which was to be my only source of income while in graduate school.

Exploring the town and the campus was fun and exciting. The university was many times larger than my former small Christian college. There I had been in a leadership position and almost everyone had been a friend or at least an acquaintance. In contrast, this huge campus was almost overwhelming. But I quickly learned my way to the buildings important for my studies.

Since Sharon had been an undergraduate at this university, she already knew many students and graciously introduced me to her numerous and diverse friends. Among these were two special men, Steve and Alan, both of whom would play a significant role in my life. Of all the graduate students introduced to me by Sharon, I was most attracted to Steve. But according to Sharon, he was "almost engaged" and thus off-limits at the time. I didn't know then, but in God's timing, Steve would become my husband.

Alan[5] was an older student in another school of the university, attending college following his military service. When I first moved in with Sharon, he stopped by to say hello to her "new roommate." He was nice looking, and quite charming. He started coming by the apartment and after a few weeks we began to date. Eventually, our relationship became intimate.

---

5 Alan is an alias, not his real name.

Six

CHANGING
DIRECTIONS

One morning in October, I awoke nauseated and soon vomited. My period was already a week late. Panicking, I called Alan. "I woke up this morning sick to my stomach and threw up. I'm a week late," I said through my tears. "I think I might be pregnant!"

"Are you sure? How can that be? We've been careful." He sounded as panicked as I felt.

"Yes, I know. But I am never late and I am never sick to my stomach in the morning. What am I going to do? I can't be pregnant and stay in school. Dr. Browning won't keep me in the program if he finds out."

"Do you want to get an abortion?" Alan asked.

"Will that take care of it?" I asked. "Whatever I need to do, I'll do it. The sooner, the better."

I felt desperate. Neither of us even mentioned the idea of getting married. We had been dating for some time but we were not talking about a future together. Abortion appeared to be the only option. In the late 60s, it was not acceptable to be single and pregnant, at least in our part of the country. More importantly, a pregnancy would certainly end my assistantship, my doctoral program, and my future career. At least that was my mindset at the time. Terms such as pro-choice and pro-life were not being used in conversations among my circle of friends. Although it seems tragic to me now, it did not occur to me that abortion not only ended a pregnancy—it also ended a life.

In the fall of 1969, abortions were not legal in my state, but they were available if you knew whom to contact. Alan knew a nurse he thought might be willing to tell us where to go. She gave him what she termed a "good and safe" resource about two hours away. He made an appointment. The cost was very high for students' budgets, so we agreed to split the fee. I had to borrow the money using a cash advance on the bank credit card that came with my new checking account. I did not have the income to pay it off quickly, so I went into debt for the first time in my life.

Alan drove me to the appointment. The office had once been a fine residence in an older part of town. We checked in, paid our money—cash only—and sat in a waiting room with several other young women. When my turn came I was ushered into an examining room.

"Hello, I'm Dr. Green," said the grey-haired man as he offered his handshake. "I'm going to take your blood pressure and pulse. Then I'm going to give you an injection which will cause you to expel the pregnancy in a few days. Is that okay with you?"

That sounded fine to me. Very simple. I had no idea what normally happened in an abortion. He gave the injection into my hip from a large vial then left me alone in the room for a few minutes. I lay there on the examining table, amazed this was so easy. Dr. Green came back and checked my vital signs. He said everything seemed okay and dismissed me. I met Alan in the waiting room and we left.

In the car, I settled into the seat, relieved the nightmare would soon be over.

"Are you okay?" Alan looked concerned as he drove us away from the old house. "I've heard it can be painful and they sometimes use a knife."

"A knife?" I said, shocked. "No. He just gave me an injection in the hip from a large vial and said the pregnancy would expel in about a week."

"Really? That's not what I expected, but if it works, that sounds a lot safer. I'm glad he used an injection rather than the alternative."

Seeking a lighter subject, we talked about the university and the upcoming football game. Then fatigue took over and I dozed for the rest of the trip.

Back at my apartment building, Alan squeezed my hand as I started to leave the car. "Let me know how things go and if you need me for anything."

"I will. He said it would be just a few days."

I anxiously waited for something to happen. After several days, I expelled a large blob of bloody tissue. Believing this completed the abortion, I assumed I was no longer pregnant. I felt no remorse; just enormous relief. It was over. Or so I thought.

In retrospect, I am amazed I did not ask questions or try to find out more about the procedure. In my naiveté, I took what I had been told at face value. It is hard to imagine in today's world of the Internet, Google, Wikipedia, drugstore pregnancy tests, and pregnancy care centers, but I had no way to confidentially find any more information. So I celebrated that I was no longer pregnant, continued my graduate classes, finished the quarter with high grades, and went home to visit my parents for Christmas vacation.

There was no need for them to know about the pregnancy. They had always been so loving and supportive, and proud of my achievements. I had never done anything outrageously wrong and always did my best to please them. After all their sacrifices to give me an outstanding education, I felt I could not disappoint them. After all, I was an adult living on my own hundreds of miles from home. No need to upset them. And anyway, it was all over.

My euphoria was short-lived. Back at school, I realized something was very wrong. I had still not started my period and I seemed to be gaining weight. Having heard from someone that birth control pills helped to regulate the menstrual cycle, I found a way to get the pills and started taking them. I began to smoke, believing that might help me lose weight. I studied hard, went on a date occasionally, and blindly hoped things would get back to normal.

I didn't see Alan much anymore. He had finished his degree in December and moved to a large city to start his first job. It was so different just seeing him a couple of weekends a month. In the meantime, I moved to a different apartment with two female graduate students. Hannah[6], a dedicated Christian, went to church every week and sang in the choir. She kept inviting Vicki and me to go to church with her, but we always declined.

Hannah heard about a new high protein/low carbohydrate diet. Since we all felt we should lose a little weight, we agreed to support one another and go on the diet for two weeks. We all lost weight; I lost ten pounds. We celebrated with hot fudge sundaes from Dairy Queen. The diet was over! Enjoying my slimmer figure, I bought some new clothes, including something to help hold in my stomach and carried on through the winter term.

A few weeks after March spring break, I awoke in the middle

---

6 Hannah and Vicki are aliases, not their real names.

of the night feeling a throbbing in my abdomen. I panicked. Something was very wrong. Even though I had not seen him in several weeks, I called Alan and told him I needed to go back to the doctor. He agreed to go with me.

Dr. Green examined me and said he could take care of the situation with another injection at no extra cost. I asked about the mass expelled from the first injection. He said I must have been pregnant with twins and aborted only one fetus.

Twins? Twin *babies*? I'd thought of that mass as just tissue. I couldn't have been carrying twins! That couldn't be possible.

If nothing happened within a week I was to come back. I told Alan what Dr. Green had said about twins and he was as disbelieving as I was. The rest of the trip back to my apartment was very quiet. Neither of us seemed to have any idea what to say.

A week passed and nothing happened. I called Alan and told him I needed to go back to the doctor. I wanted to go on Friday when I had no classes, but he could not go with me that day. He gave me the directions and I drove myself to the clinic. The doctor assured me I was not quite ready but that everything would be all right.

"What do you mean?" I asked. "What am I to do?"

"Come back in a few days and I'll take care of it," the doctor instructed. Not realizing he meant he would take care of the fetus, I left the old house.

During the two-hour drive back to my apartment, I considered the parting instruction. With exams coming up the following week, I wondered when I could return to the doctor. But I pushed the whole problem to the back of my mind and enjoyed the fresh white blossoms of the dogwood trees scattered among the spring green of new leaves.

Oh my goodness, I thought. It had been an entire year since the previous April when I had first seen the beauty of the white dogwoods at my graduate school interview. I had been so innocent then. How had I gotten into such a mess?

⁕

An invitation to a cookout on Saturday night was a welcome diversion. The loose clothes then in fashion and my recent weight loss camouflaged my expanding waistline. As far as I knew, no one suspected I might be pregnant. Not feeling well, I asked my date to take me home early. I made it to the bathroom just in time to regurgitate my dinner.

Exhausted, I went to bed only to wake about midnight with severe cramps and a heavy discharge. "This might be the end of all this," I thought. I was so uncomfortable that I couldn't go back to sleep. I alternated lying on the couch and walking around, but could not rest. I felt extremely ill and began to think I had food poisoning or a bad case of stomach flu. Knowing nothing about labor, I did not connect my condition with how sick I felt. Regarding the pregnancy, I thought I would probably expel something as I had done the first time when the injection took effect.

After a long sleepless night, I heard Hannah's alarm clock ring at six o'clock the next morning. "Maybe she can take me to the Student Health Center," I thought. I knocked on her bedroom door. When she answered, I realized she was dressing to go to church.

"Hannah, I'm really sick. I think I might have food poisoning or a stomach virus. I hate to ask, but I think I need to see a doctor. Can you take me to the Student Health Clinic before you go to church?"

Noticing my ashen face and the pain in my expression, she immediately responded. "Yes, of course. I'll be glad to and it's on my way. I'm so sorry you are sick. Maybe they can give you something to make you feel better. Get on some clothes and we can go right now. I'll be ready to go when you are."

"Vicki, Bette's sick and I'm taking her to the clinic. We'll see you later," she called to our other roommate who was still in bed as we went out the door.

The Student Health Center was on campus, not too far from our apartment. A nurse and a physician assistant were on duty. No one else was in the entry room. The PA sat down next to me and asked why I had come. I told them about regurgitating my dinner the night before, the severe stomach pain, and that I thought was hemorrhaging.

"Elizabeth, may I feel your stomach?" the PA asked. I nodded yes. As he placed his hand on my abdomen, his chin dropped and he drew back his hand in surprise. "Wait a minute. There's movement in there! Are you pregnant? I think you are in labor!"

"How can that be? I can't be in labor. I'm supposed to be expelling this pregnancy!"

"You mean you have tried to abort?" he asked.

I nodded my head and whispered, "Yes."

He turned to Hannah. "You need to take her to the emergency room immediately."

"I didn't know she was pregnant," Hannah said, her eyes wide. "Can you call an ambulance for her?"

"You can get her there faster," he urged. "Do you know where it is? You need to go right now."

Hannah nodded yes, then turned to me. "Okay, Bette. We're going to the emergency room!"

Seven

NEW BIRTH

*B*undled into Hannah's car again, I felt the vehicle speeding down the street. Fortunately, the hospital was just a few blocks away. I am sure Hannah was praying we would get there in time. She told me she had seen my abdomen moving at the clinic. She was shocked since she had no idea I was pregnant.

At the hospital, Hannah checked me in. They rushed me upstairs in a wheelchair. I was shocked to be on the way to labor and delivery. Someone helped me onto a gurney and pushed me down the hall. I soon found myself in a room with several other women. Most of them were moaning, apparently under full anesthesia, the common practice for birthing pain control at that time. I, however, was fully awake and in pain. A nurse examined me and asked the date of my last period.

"Six months!" she repeated incredulously. She left and quickly returned with a doctor. I heard her say, "It's breech!" I did not know what that meant, but she seemed concerned. They stayed with me and before I realized what was happening, the doctor held up a very small baby. A tiny being had come out of me. Until that moment, I had not acknowledged the idea I was having a baby, a *live* baby.

The doctor quickly thrust the tiny body into the waiting arms of the nurse. "Get this baby to neonatal. Maybe we can save it!"

The enormity of what had just happened hit me. I became hysterical, screaming over and over, "I never meant to have a baby who was not wanted!" They tried to quiet me, but I could not be comforted. What I did not realize at the time was that this baby *was* wanted, and through my roommate's quick action in getting me to the clinic and then the emergency room, God had miraculously spared the baby's life, and possibly mine as well.

⚜

Sometime later I awoke in a hospital room. I have no memory of leaving the delivery room. The doctor must have ordered something to calm my hysteria. It was late Sunday morning, April 19, 1970. I hurried to the bathroom. To my surprise, I expelled what appeared to be an umbilical cord and maybe a placenta. Was this from the baby I had just birthed? Knowing so little about the process, I thought it might be. I was so traumatized by the whole experience, and now this discharged substance, I just withdrew from it all. Typical for an introvert, I did not tell anyone about this strange occurrence or ask what it was about.

In retrospect, I am certain any licensed doctor would have made sure to deliver the baby's afterbirth. Could this have been left from the twin aborted following the first procedure? I suspect it was, but will never know for certain.

I broke down and sobbed. I felt devastated. Over the past twelve months I had torn down all the high personal standards I had held for myself in the first twenty-one years of my life and now I had birthed a baby. *A baby!*

What in the world would I do now?

⚜

After Hannah checked me in at the emergency room, she watched incredulously, shaking her head with deep concern for me and the baby as I disappeared behind the elevator doors on the way to labor and delivery. Later she told me she left her name and our apartment phone number with the ER clerk and asked to be called when I was placed in a room, then she went to her car.

She felt exhausted from the surprise events of the early morning, overwhelmed with the knowledge of her roommate's attempted abortion and forthcoming birth. The Lord filled her heart with the need to meditate on His Word and pray for the baby and me, praying we both would be okay. Sitting in her car in the hospital parking lot, she read her Bible and lifted up her petitions in prayer to the Lord. She wished she could do more. Not knowing what her role should be, she decided not to go to church, but to go to the apartment in case there was a call.

At that moment, Hannah was the only person in the world other than the clinic and hospital staff who knew her roommate was at the hospital in the throes of childbirth for a baby she had tried to abort. Her role, God-given, was clearly communicated: to meditate on His Word and to pray for the survival and well-being of the baby, and for me, the resistant mother, she asked for survival, repentance, forgiveness, and salvation through the Lord Jesus Christ.

Thank you, thank you, Hannah, for your obedience and prayerful petitions at that critical time so long ago. Your prayers have been answered in abundance.

Vicki expectantly met Hannah at the apartment door. "Where's Bette?"

"She's at the hospital—having a baby!"

"What? A baby?" Her mouth dropped open. "You must be kidding!" She sat down quickly, stunned from Hannah's news. "How could she be pregnant and we didn't know it? We live in the same apartment! She didn't look pregnant, especially after our two-week diet last month. And she lost the most weight—ten pounds!"

"I know, I'm still in shock. I had no idea she was pregnant and in labor until the PA at the Student Health Clinic realized it and sent us on to the emergency room."

"Do you know how she is? Have you talked with her?"

"No, it's probably too early. I came home to wait for a call from the hospital."

About an hour later, the phone rang. Hannah ran to answer it. "Hello!"

"Is this Hannah Smith?"

"Yes, it is. Is this the hospital?"

"Yes, this is the emergency room clerk. I was told to call and give you the status on Elizabeth Jones. She is resting comfortably in room #2214 and her baby is being cared for in the neonatal unit."

She thanked the clerk for calling, hung up, and turned to Vicki with a big smile. "That was the hospital. Praise the Lord, Bette's in a room and the baby is in neonatal. It sounds like they're both okay."

❧

The phone rang in my room and interrupted my anxious thoughts.

"Hi, how are you doing?" Hannah's kind voice was good to hear.

"I'm okay. The baby was born breech and was rushed to neonatal. It was about three months premature and very tiny."

"Was it a boy or a girl?"

"I—I don't know. I just saw it briefly when the doctor held it up. I don't know anything else."

"I see." She paused. "Is there anything I can do for you?"

"Oh, yes!" My practicality took over. I hadn't brought anything with me other than what I was wearing with no thought about being hospitalized. "Can you bring my caftan, my Dr. Scholl's sandals, my hairbrush, my hairclip, and—" I started to tear up, and my voice shook. "—and thank you for getting me here this morning. The baby was born not long after they took me upstairs, about nine o'clock, I guess. I don't think I could have made it on my own. I'm so sorry. I had no idea it would happen this way."

"You're most welcome. Vickie and I had no idea either. I'm just glad you are okay. I'll bring those things after lunch. Oh, do you want me to call Alan?"

"Would you mind? He needs to know what's happened. I'm sure I can't make a long distance call from here. Just give him the hospital phone number and my room. Leave a message if he doesn't answer. He's probably out of town."

Hannah brought my things and made sure I was all right. After she left, I put on my sandals and the bright green and black floor-length caftan I used as a robe and started to walk around. An unexpected thought popped into my mind. *Where is the baby?*

This sudden interest in seeing it took me by surprise. After delivery, they had moved me to the post-operative ward of the hospital instead of maternity. I went upstairs to the maternity ward and found the nursery. In my boldly colored garb and long blonde hair, I was in stark contrast to the pastel pink-and-blue-clad mothers visiting with family and friends in front of the nursery window. I looked at all the babies but did not see one tiny enough to be mine. Then I realized a premature baby would not be there.

I tried to find neonatal, but could not bring myself to ask anyone for directions. As I shuffled around the halls, wondering what the baby looked like, it became clear to me that it might be unsettling to see. I was a graduate student in psychology and knew the bond between mother and child formed most strongly soon after birth. Seeing the baby would only intensify this maternal feeling I was beginning to recognize within me.

I had no means of caring for a baby by myself. Alan had not been around very much since December after he'd graduated and had moved to start his new job in the city. In fact, I had not seen him at all in the last two months except for the first return trip to the abortionist. I saw no future there. And even if there had been a future for us, our differences in faith, although not currently in evidence—mine Christian, his Jewish—loomed large in my mind. I was also convinced marrying "for the sake of the baby" would not guarantee a good marriage or a good environment for a child. I had seen several negative examples while in college.

It's not a good idea to see the baby, I told myself. *What if I did get attached? What then? An attachment would only complicate things and make everything harder to deal with.* Returning to my room, I walked by the nursery again. I looked longingly at the families crowded around the big window. I hoped someday I'd be excited to see my baby through a nursery window. Tearing up again, I rushed on to my room.

That afternoon a social worker came to talk with me. She suggested that if I was not willing to take care of the baby, the Department of Family and Children's Services (DFACS) could take custody and make the child available for adoption when it was ready to leave the hospital. There were papers to sign to transfer parental rights. Both the father and I, if possible, would need to come to the DFACS office and fill out family historical information for potential adoptive parents. She said I could think it over. But I already knew my decision. I could see no other alternative. I signed the papers so the baby could be adopted.

Late that evening Alan called. Hannah had left the message to call me at the hospital. He said he had been in Florida for a wedding. He asked if I had gone back to the doctor the third time and wondered what had gone wrong. I recounted the events of the previous forty-eight hours. I concluded with, "The baby was born alive."

"A baby? Alive?" he said in disbelief.

"Yes. They took it away quickly to try to save its life," I said. "It's in neonatal somewhere. I tried to find that department on my own, but didn't ask anyone if I could see the baby."

He was quiet for a few seconds. "I'll come over first thing in the morning. I've been driving most of the day. I've got to get some sleep."

The next morning, I had hardly finished breakfast when an anxious-looking Alan rushed into the room and sat on the edge of the chair next to the bed. "How could this have happened?"

"The doctor told me to come back in a few days or if something started to happen, but I couldn't have made it there on my own. I don't think I could have made it here without Hannah driving me."

"What will happen to the baby?"

"I have signed papers for it to be adopted."

He looked disappointed. "You've already signed the papers?"

"What else could I do?"

"Well, I don't know. I just thought we might have talked about it first." Alan's voice trailed off. He gazed at me wistfully. "This could be complicated."

He paused to think and then began to put his thoughts into words. "In the last two months I've been dating some other women. I had begun to think we wouldn't be seeing each other anymore, especially since we thought the first injection had ended the pregnancy. But the baby changes things."

I didn't know how to respond to his last statement and changed the subject. After talking for a while about the need to give family history to DFACS, he stood to leave and said he would be in touch.

Decades later, I learned that due to the baby's birth Alan had actually considered marriage to me. Had I realized the transfer of parental rights was not final at that time I could have reversed my decision to place the baby for adoption. But at the time I did not know either of those things.

Eight

POSTPARTUM

The next day, as I prepared to leave the hospital room, I glanced out the window. The row of pink dogwoods in front of the building had burst into bloom. How beautiful! The array of lovely blossoms brightened my spirits and diverted my thoughts for a few moments from the enormity of what had happened since Saturday night.

A nurse arrived with a wheelchair. "Are you ready?" She motioned for me to sit in the chair. Pushing me toward the elevator, she chatted about the beautiful spring day. At the checkout area, a stern looking middle-aged woman, Ms. Harris, according to her name plate, waited at the payment window.

"Good morning. May I help you?"

"Yes, please. I'm Elizabeth Jones, checking out."

"Let me find your account." She flipped through a pile of papers and pulled out several pages. "Elizabeth, you have quite a large balance on your account and no insurance to cover your charges. Who will be responsible for your hospital bill?"

"I will be, but I will not be able to pay anything until my next paycheck."

"Elizabeth, if you cannot pay now we will need to get in touch with your parents."

I could not let that happen.

"Ms. Harris, my parents live in another state. I am a legal adult and not dependent upon them. I will find a way to pay this bill." I stood up from the wheel chair and tried to look as mature as possible in my sweater, bell-bottom jeans, and blond ponytail. "My parents are not responsible for me. The hospital has no right to contact them."

I looked down at the paperwork she slid through the window opening. There was my name, and below it, "Baby Boy Jones." I took a deep breath and held onto the counter to steady myself for a moment. My knees shook and I felt faint. No one had mentioned the baby's gender. Until that moment I did not know it was a boy.

"Thank you, Ms. Harris," I said shakily. "I'll be back in two days with a partial payment."

Exhausted emotionally and physically, I rode back to the apartment with Hannah and went to bed. My roommates were both graduate students in counseling, but they didn't know what to say to me, nor did I know what to say to them. So we did not talk at all about the surprise birth.

The next day, I struggled to get up. At discharge I had asked the doctor for a written excuse for the classes and exams I had missed. He said I should rest a couple more days before I returned to my normal routine. Pale-faced and weak, I ignored his advice and went back to class. I talked to my professors about how to make up what I had missed, but left early and went back to bed. The doctor was right—I would need a few more days to recover my energy and productivity. I stayed out of class the following day and asked help from my classmates for lecture notes on the days I had missed because of my hospitalization.

Due to missed lectures, exams, and late research papers in two courses, I learned I would have to request permission for "Incomplete" status and fulfill the requirements during the summer term. My major professor was supportive and made the requests on my behalf. He agreed to continue my research assistantship over the summer and for the next year on condition that I complete and present the research study already accepted by the national conference scheduled the following month.

By the end of the quarter, I had made up all the exams I had missed and avoided an Incomplete in one class. I also completed the research paper for Dr. Browning's assistantship and presented it at the conference. However, a second class completion hinged on a satisfactory grade on a sophisticated statistical analysis and report. I planned to complete the research report over the summer.

Soon after the baby's birth, Alan took a day off from his job and went with me to the DFACS office to document our family histories. Alan was very considerate and told me he would do everything he could to take care of the hospital bills, but he would appreciate any amount I could contribute. I agreed. The bill was much larger than either of us had envisioned, but he was true to his word. He had to take out a loan, delay plans for new housing and other purchases, but he paid all the hospital expenses except a small portion from my meager resources.

Six weeks after the birth, I went to my postpartum appointment with the doctor who had delivered the baby. He was much kinder than he had been in the hospital. I suppose he had been quite upset with me at delivery since the premature birth was due to an attempted abortion.

"I've been told the baby's father visited you in the hospital and was with you at the Department of Family and Children's

Services' office to give family history information." He leaned forward and looked me in the eyes. "I've seen a lot of situations with babies in my time—some good, some bad. It appears you care for each other. In your case, I would encourage you to reconsider your decision for adoption. Marry this man who cares for you, and give your child a home."

"I don't see how that could work," I said, shaking my head. "I have thought a lot about the options. Marriage is just not right for us and I don't think it's in the best interest of the baby."

Looking back after many decades, it is clear God had already prepared loving parents and a wonderful home for our child, a home with a stable environment and close-knit extended family far beyond what Alan and I could have provided.

The end of the spring term brought a welcome respite at my parents' home and the chance to attend my brother's high school graduation. The relaxed atmosphere was short-lived, however, due to a phone call from Hannah.

"Bette, I'm so sorry for interrupting your visit with your family, but the DFACS office has called trying to locate you. I told them you were visiting relatives in Florida and would not be back for another week."

"Oh, dear! Did they say why they were calling?"

"No, they would not tell me anything; only that it was extremely important for you to call back. I have the number and the name of the person you are to talk to."

I looked around the phone table and found some note paper and a pencil.

"Okay, Hannah, I'm ready to write it down."

As I put down the pencil, I could feel anxiety building inside me. "Oh, Hannah, I was just beginning to relax. It's so good to be at home. But thanks for calling and letting me know about this. I'll see you when I get back."

I thought it best to call DFACS elsewhere rather than at home. There were no cell phones then—my only option was to use a pay phone. I gathered up all the change I had and hoped it would cover the long-distance call. I drove to a shopping center and found a pay phone in a booth where I could sit down for a private conversation and made the call.

"DFACS Office," the voice at the other end answered. "How may I help you?"

"Hello, this is Elizabeth Jones. I had a message to call your office."

"One moment, please."

A pleasant voice said, "Hello, is this Elizabeth?"

"Yes, it is."

"That's good. I'm glad to talk to you. Your roommate said you were out of town. I'm Mrs. Brown, a social worker with DFACS. I want to give you an update on Baby Boy Jones. He has done remarkably well in the hospital. His fingernails have grown in, he's alert and notices everything around him."

I tried to absorb what she was saying. *Fingernails? I didn't know that premature babies did not have fingernails.* "That sounds good. I'm glad he has done well," I responded.

"Yes, he has. Few babies as small and premature as he was survive. The reason I am calling is that the baby has gained almost three pounds! He is up to five pounds, six ounces."

"That's still so small."

"Yes, but medically he is ready to be discharged to foster care until he is placed for adoption." She paused. "Is that still your intent?"

"Yes, I think it is the best thing for the baby and for me. I have no way to support a child."

"Okay, it sounds like that is the best decision for you and the baby. Since that is still what you want for the child, you must come in right away to the DFACS office and sign the papers to relinquish your parental rights so he can be discharged to foster care."

"Oh, I thought I had already done that."

"That's what must be affirmed before foster care placement. When can you come in?"

"I'm sorry but I am visiting relatives in Florida and rode down here with friends. I'll have to check with them to see how soon they can leave. I will let you know as soon as I return. Hopefully we can leave shortly."

"Please call so I will know when to expect you. Just ask for Mrs. Brown."

Four days later, I drove to the DFACS building and signed the required papers.

After another month Mrs. Brown called again to tell me a couple wanted to adopt the baby and I must come to the office again to sign the permanent papers to release him for adoption. The child was three months old and had defied the odds against survival. It was finally all over. As was common at that time, I was given no input in the placement process. I did not see the baby nor meet the prospective parents.

It was a closed adoption. No information and no contact—for the next forty years.

Nine

COUNSEL,
CONVERSATIONS,
AND REVELATIONS

*S*oon after meeting Michael the first time, I knew I could no longer keep that part of my life in the past. With my heart racing about revealing my long-hidden secret, I walked into the church office to meet with Dr. Matt, a trusted pastor friend. I found him waiting for me in the lobby.

"Hi, Matt. Thanks for taking time to meet with me."

"Hello, Bette. It's so good to see you." He reached out his hand and leaned over to give me a grandfatherly kiss on the cheek, as was his custom.

I had made the appointment because Steve and I agreed that professional counseling would be essential for me in order to put this major event in perspective and also to get feedback on how the church might view this revelation. At that time I was a deacon in our church and had recently been elected an elder with my term beginning in the coming year.

Dr. Matt was a retired senior minister in his eighties, a very wise and gifted counselor, with a lifetime of experience in church politics. He had counseled both my husband and me in times past, and I trusted him. Before we went to Michael's church to hear him sing, I felt I needed his wisdom, and without knowing what was troubling me, he had immediately agreed to see me.

Matt led me to a small, modestly furnished office used by part-time staff. We sat in chairs facing each other. "What brings you here today?" His warm welcome helped to put me at ease.

"Matt, just to let you know up front, it's not a problem with our marriage or our sons." I smiled as I gathered my thoughts. "It dates back before we were married. I have a very unusual situation and I need your wisdom. I think you'll see that you have a unique perspective on what I'm about to tell you."

He sat quietly, listening intently, his full attention on me as I shared all the details. He asked about Michael's age and marital status. When I answered that Michael had children, Matt exclaimed, "So you are a grandmother!" Then he leaned toward me and took my hand. "Bette, this is a great blessing, one to be celebrated, and for which to be grateful to God." With his other hand, he patted the top of mine.

Inwardly, I felt greatly relieved and grateful for his positive, non-judgmental response.

"It is wonderful that Michael had the blessing of his parents to pursue finding you, and this first meeting has gone so well. I think his purpose of finding his birth-mother to make sure she was a Christian is also a tremendous blessing." He paused and shook his head. "I have been counseling for many, many years and have never heard a story quite like this."

Matt was familiar with adoption. He and his first wife had adopted two children, then she had died when the children were quite young. He and his current wife had three natural children. He told me his adopted children had not attempted to contact their birth families and did not plan to do so.

"Bette," he said clearly and firmly, looking straight into my eyes, "I feel this blessing has been given to you to share, to give testimony to the providence of God and His redeeming grace. I'm going to challenge you to resolve not to hide, but to proclaim this story and to pray for strength and courage to do so." He straightened up and cleared his throat. "As far as the church is concerned, I feel certain there will be no repercussions *when*— not *if*—you make this public." He smiled. "After all, the church is in the business of loving and forgiving in the example of Christ."

"Matt, that's a lot more than what I expected you to say." That was an understatement! His words took my breath away. "It's quite a challenge to think about. I was just hoping you would say it was okay to be an elder with this in my past. I am afraid of being exposed by just being seen with Michael at his church. How can I possibly talk about this publically?"

"You'll be given the strength and courage to tell it. I feel sure you will." He reached to hold both my hands in his. "Let me pray for you and your family; especially your sons when they are told."

His voice was tender and comforting as he prayed. My eyes overflowed with tears, grateful for this wonderful man of God and his encouraging yet challenging counsel. Already I felt stronger and more secure about meeting Michael at his church. But talking about this to other people? I was not so sure about accepting that challenge.

Paul, our Associate Pastor, was especially close to both our sons. He had known them since their childhood when he came to our church as youth pastor. They each had a standing invitation for lunch with him at Johnny's BBQ anytime they were in town.

Although Dr. Matt was certainly qualified to speak to the possible response of the church, I felt the need for confirmation from a current church pastor. I was still quite concerned about my upcoming ordination as an elder and was willing to step down rather than cause embarrassment to the church.

As I drove to my counseling appointment with Paul, I was more nervous about facing him than I had been Dr. Matt. As close as Paul was to our sons, in the twenty-five years I had known him I had never discussed personal matters with him.

Walking into his big office was like entering a library. Paul was an avid reader and books were stacked high on all sides.

"Bette, how good to see you!" His broad smile and hearty two-handed clasp welcomed me and calmed my anxiety. "Please sit down." He motioned to one of the upholstered chairs in front of his desk as he sat in the other. "I'm so glad you came by. What's on your mind?"

Attempting to seem casual, I brought up some church matters for discussion and then told him the latest updates about Mark and Clark.

"Paul, I do have something else to tell you about. Don't worry, it's nothing bad, but it does have to do with our family." I swallowed hard, and then launched into my real topic.

Paul's eyes grew wide as I talked. He was obviously surprised but also quite impacted by my story.

"Bette, this is a story I would never have believed to be true had I not heard it directly from you. It is truly remarkable. There is so much evidence of the direct hand of God in your son's survival and his search for you and your response." He appeared to choose his words carefully. "I definitely give you my blessing for going public if and when you are ready. As far as the church is concerned, I feel strongly that your unplanned pregnancy as a single woman forty years ago is not going to cause a problem with the church or your ordination as an elder."

Paul then told me a story of his own. Unknown to me and perhaps to most of our congregation, his parents had both been married previously and each had a son from the prior marriage. Growing up, Paul did not know that his mother's son, who lived with his family, was a half-brother. His father's son by his first marriage, however, lived far away with his father's first wife.

"Bette, one of the great regrets of my life is that I did not get to know my other half-brother." He had tears in his eyes. "I saw him only two or three times in my life, and now he has passed on."

He took my hand in both of his. "Here's my point in telling you about my family. From my own experience, I feel it is very important and meaningful that your sons not only know their half-brother, but build a relationship with him. I understand how difficult this will be for you because I know how close you all are. You know I love your sons. After all, I've half-raised them." He grinned warmly. "I have walked alongside them as they have grown into fine men. Let's pray right now that the Lord will prepare them for this revelation."

After he prayed we walked to the office door. With his hand on the doorknob and a big smile on his face, he said, "I look forward to hearing you tell this story publically. I can't wait for the book and the movie."

I laughed. "Don't hold your breath!"

It was time to call my friend, Stephi, who had told me about meeting her oldest granddaughter as an adult. Unknowingly, she had given me godly counsel about how to handle my first meeting with Michael. She had also imparted hope that such a reunion could work out well. In our phone conversation she had taken my story at face value. Now she was shocked to learn that the person who had heard from her long-lost son was actually me!

"Bette," she said excitedly, "you need to share your experience. It is a powerful story of redemption." I thanked her for her advice and encouragement. I told her I would keep in touch and update her periodically.

❖

Michael told me his parents were very pleased he had found me and the reunion had gone well. He said his mother, Connie, wanted to talk with me. He asked me to call her and gave me the phone number. A few days after my husband and I met Michael's children, I called Connie. *This is so unusual,* I thought as I entered the number. *How do you talk to the woman who raised your son?*

She made it easy. "The first thing I have wanted to say to you if I ever had the opportunity," she began, "is thank you! Michael has been the light of my life. He's my heart." I could sense her excitement and sincerity.

Connie told me they had received the call from DFACS about a baby who had been in the hospital for two months, then in foster care for a month, and was just back to the foster home after a short stay in the hospital. The social worker said he was ready for adoption and they could see him if they were interested in adopting. She asked her husband, Jesse, if he wanted to go.

"Get ready. We're going!" he told her.

"The moment I saw him and his big blue eyes," she said, "I fell in love with him. Jesse took one look at him, turned to me and said, 'That's my boy!' He was a wonderful child to raise—bright, personable, and loving—but with a strong spirit." She was obviously proud of her son. "Though he had mild cerebral palsy and an improperly developed heel requiring leg braces, he really pushed himself to do things. At some point he decided not to wear the braces anymore and he did fine without them.

"He played several sports, and was motivated to do well in them," she continued. "He was also very musical. He had a strong voice, loved to sing, and learned to play the piano and guitar."

I wanted to say something, but she kept talking and I continued taking notes.

"He never met a stranger and knew many people in the community. We sent him to a private academy in our town. He was very smart, a really good student. He graduated a year early and earned a scholarship for college."

Connie's voice softened. "I'm so glad he has found you. Early on we let him know he was adopted. We told him the story of when we came to see him, and that we had chosen him."

I already knew some of the story. Michael had told me how his father recounted it each time the family drove into the town where the foster care home was located. He would say, "I remember the day we turned this corner on the way to see you for the first time. Boy, I've been loving you a long time."

Connie continued, "Michael always had a deep longing to connect with his birth parents and I am very glad to share him with you. I am not threatened, just grateful that in the midst of the circumstances of his birth, you placed him for adoption. It takes a rare woman to give up the child she has carried in her womb."

Her statement wrenched my heart. The sentiment sounded so noble compared to my self-serving, desperate decision to place the baby for adoption following the failed abortion. Feeling it was not appropriate in this conversation, I resisted the urge to reveal the facts as I had with Michael. Instead, I prayed silently, *Lord, thank you that my desires were not granted. Thank you for overriding my decision and answering this special couple's prayers for a child to raise.*

Connie told me she had experienced nine miscarriages in nine years of marriage. Finally, the doctors had told her she could not carry a baby to full term. She and Jesse had given up on being parents until they were offered adoption. They jumped at the chance.

"Jesse and I would like to meet you and your husband," she said. "I'll ask Michael to arrange a meeting."

"We would love to meet you," I replied. "My husband and I agree you have been incredible parents and have raised a very fine man. I'm humbled to have been able to contribute part of the 'raw material.'"

Given my situation at the time of his birth I realized once again I could never have provided the physical care, parental upbringing, stable family, and especially the spiritual environment in which they had nurtured Michael, molding him into the fine man he was today.

That conversation went so well! It was a testimony to Connie's confidence in her role as a mother, her faith in the Lord, and her God-given ability to parent a child like Michael. We would never have talked if she had been insecure and defensive about her status as an adoptive mother.

I was amazed at the courage of Connie and Jesse to take home a tiny five-pound baby boy still in ill health at three months of age. Michael had told us of his adoptive grandfather's response to seeing the new baby for the first time. He'd left the house shaking his head. "I'll give him a week. He'll never make it."

❧

Shortly after my conversation with Connie, I was provided a dramatic, real-life illustration of Connie and Jesse's first days at home with Michael.

Steve and I were volunteering at our church with Safe Havens, a program that works with the Juvenile Courts and DFACS to provide a safe, controlled environment for parents to spend time with their children who had been removed from their homes for various reasons. By participating in supervised visitations, parenting classes, and meeting other criteria, parents could earn the privilege of bringing their children back into their homes.

On that particular Saturday morning, I supervised a young single mother and her three children—two girls, five- and three-years-old, and a three-week-old boy. The baby had been born two months premature while the mother was in jail, and now weighed only five pounds.

Before that day, Safe Havens had never worked with the parent of a baby that young. I had only seen Michael at the moment of his birth. I had never held him or hugged him until meeting him as an adult. When I held the tiny baby boy at Safe Havens, I was able to experience what it might have been like when Michael was finally ready to go home with his new parents.

As I held that very small bundle, the enormity of adopting a premature baby in 1970 became very real for me. How could I possibly have handled the challenge of caring for such a tiny child, either single or married to Michael's father? What a risk Connie and Jesse assumed given his poor health. But none of those negatives were considered in their decision. Their faith gave them the courage and they jumped at the chance to have a child. They trusted the Lord for His provision and praised Him for answering their fervent prayers—prayers that spanned nine heart-breaking miscarriages.

Michael was placed with a couple who had the spiritual underpinning to believe God answered prayers. Could it be God had preserved Michael's life through all the attempts to end it in order to provide a son for this godly couple?

Lord, thank you that my desires were not granted. Thank you for overriding my decision and answering this special couple's prayers for a child to love.

Ten

CONNECTING THE BROTHERS

The call from Michael had come near the end of our younger son's military deployment in the Indian Ocean on the USS Peleliu, a small naval carrier called an amphibious assault vessel. Onboard were U.S. Marine Corps helicopters and Harrier jets, all vertical take-off aircraft, and a large cadre of combat Marine ground troops.

Clark was a Captain in the U.S. Marine Corps and a CH-53E Super Stallion helicopter pilot. The CH-53 is the largest U.S. military helicopter aloft and is capable of carrying an all-terrain vehicle with fully-equipped Marine troops into combat. In the humanitarian relief effort for Pakistan following devastating floods during the summer of 2010, our son's aircraft, along with other helicopters, had carried food, building materials, and sometimes transported more than 90 Pakistani refugees to safety.

My husband, our older son, Mark, and I had been invited, along with 200 other civilian family members of the deployed Marines and Naval personnel on the USS Peleliu, for a "Tiger Cruise." We were to board the ship at Pearl Harbor, Hawaii, and join our son for a weeklong voyage to San Diego, California, the last leg of the deployment.

Even with our excitement and anticipation, we almost missed

the trip. We had two stops on our cross-country itinerary from Atlanta to Honolulu. Late departure from Atlanta caused us to miss our first connecting flight out of Salt Lake City. There were no airline personnel at the desk, but we quickly called on our cell phones for alternative flights. Almost like magic, an airline agent appeared, walking down the concourse. I frantically hailed him. He asked if he could help as he walked to an empty console. I told him our situation, and he said the airline would put us up for the night and book us on the first flight in the morning.

"No, no, no, you don't understand!" I said, nearly in tears. "We have to be in Pearl Harbor in the morning to join our Marine son aboard the USS Peleliu at 07:15. We're going to get to go on the final leg of his deployment to San Diego. The ship will not wait for us!"

"Okay, I see what you mean," he said calmingly. "Let me have your tickets and I'll see what we can do. We have to get you to Los Angeles before the last flight leaves for Hawaii. We have to see where your bags are, too."

He logged into the computer console and went to work. In a remarkably short time he had a new itinerary for us. "Here you are," he said with a smile as he handed us new boarding passes. "You will be on a small jet with little space for baggage in the cabin, but do not let them check your carry-on because you will have very little time to change planes in Los Angeles to the Hawaii-bound flight. Good luck, and Semper Fi!"

We thanked him profusely. He started to walk away. "Oh," he said as an afterthought, "if you have time to see the USS Arizona memorial in Pearl Harbor, look on the list of those entombed in the ship for the name Byron Mason, my uncle and my namesake. It was a pleasure to serve you. Please thank your son for his service."

As we gathered our belongings and started to leave, I looked back. Our benefactor was nowhere to be seen. *Who was that man?*

We called Clark to tell him we would be late getting to Honolulu. Waiting for our substitute flight, we ate some sandwiches. Even after boarding, the plane remained at the gate for an extended time. I prayed the whole length of the flight for the Lord to get us to Honolulu in time. We landed and pulled into our gate in Los Angeles just as our flight to Hawaii was backing away from the next gate. "Oh, no!" we all exclaimed in unison.

Mark jumped to his feet as soon as the seatbelt sign went off and was at the head of the line getting off. He raced to the desk, wild-eyed, and almost screamed to the agent, "That's our flight to Honolulu that just left!"

"Calm down. What's your name?"

"Mark Noble. My parents will be off in a minute."

"I think we have you covered. One of our agents called from Salt Lake City and said if there was any problem with your connection here, we were to book you on another airline. We have you on the very last flight to Hawaii out of this airport tonight." He handed Mark three tickets, shaking his head in disbelief. "Lucky for you—this flight almost never has available seats. You'll need to get upstairs to the other airline's boarding area, Gate B14. The escalator is right over there."

By that time Steve and I had caught up with Mark. He was so excited he could hardly talk. "Mom! Dad! They have us taken care of!" He waved something in the air as he tried to catch his breath. "Here are our boarding passes on a flight with another airline. It leaves in an hour."

"You're kidding!" Steve said as he put his phone away. "I was just about to call Clark and tell him we would see him in San Diego in a week."

Tears running down my cheeks, I prayed, *Dear Lord, this is overwhelming. Thank you for your unbelievable graciousness to our family. Thank you for answering our prayers!*

I dabbed my eyes and beamed a big smile at Steve and Mark. "Let's grab a sandwich and find that gate. We're going to Hawaii!"

About midnight local time, almost 24 hours after leaving home, we arrived in Honolulu in the middle of a thunderstorm. There was Clark at the gate to welcome us, beaming from ear to ear. What a joy to see and hug him after seven long months!

Clark had a taxi waiting to take us to the Navy Lodge hotel for a few hours' sleep before we were to ship out. Luckily, the Lodge had a fully-equipped store with all the necessities—including flip-flops and beach towels—for military personnel arriving without baggage. Steve and Mark had packed everything in their checked luggage and had nothing for the voyage. Thankfully, I had all I needed in my carry-on bag. We "slept fast" for about three hours then readied ourselves to board ship.

In the pre-dawn rain at Pearl Harbor, the USS Peleliu loomed large and gray in its mooring, a huge lighted numeral "5" on its tower.

"There it is—the Iron Nickel," Clark said with evident pride, using the ship's military nickname.

We boarded with over 200 other civilian family members. Clark led us to our assigned quarters. I was in a four-bunk cabin with three other mothers of officers and a sister on a cot in the middle of the floor. Very cozy! Steve was assigned a bunk in Clark's cabin with two other pilots and Mark was down the hall.

After a quick breakfast in the Officer's Wardrobe Mess, the dining facility, we went on deck. As the ship slowly pulled away from the dock, we had the unique experience of passing the lighted USS Arizona Memorial in the mist. It had been exactly 69 years and three days since that fateful day in 1941 when our country was attacked by the Japanese, bringing the United States into WWII.

We attended an orientation for all helicopter pilot "Tigers" (family members on the cruise) in the comfortable Ready Room and were given a schedule of activities. Clark was relieved of much of his duty that first day. He took us on a tour of the ship, including the flight deck where his helicopter—Capt. C. B. Noble on the side door—was securely chained. Following a wonderful dinner, after almost no sleep the night before, I excused myself, crawled into my bunk with my clothes on and slept for thirteen hours.

Early the next morning I padded down the dimly lit co-ed corridor in my crocs and robe on the way to the cramped female head (two-person community bathroom and shower). The community bathroom reminded me of my freshman year in college. I was so young then, so naïve. That was before I became a wife and mother. Now here I was on a navy ship sharing the last week of my son's deployment before welcoming him home for Christmas.

Fears crowded in to overshadow my joy. As I flip-flopped back to my small cabin I was very much aware that I was no longer a college co-ed, but the mother of—not two, but three—grown men. I would soon have one of the toughest tasks I'd ever faced—telling my precious boys about Michael. Dressing for the day, I prayed for courage. What would my sons think of me when I told them I had been pregnant out of wedlock, I had tried unsuccessfully to abort the baby, and most startling of all, they had a half-brother I had placed for adoption?

Steve and I had agreed our sons should not be told about Michael until a face-to-face family time could be arranged with all four of us. Clark was still on duty while aboard ship. We had no private place to talk. So our plan was to wait until we were ashore.

Our time sailing the open Pacific Ocean from Hawaii to San Diego was packed with adventure—air shows from the flight deck, tours of the ship's fully-equipped hospital, demonstrations of secure remote internet systems in the field, a 5-K walk/run on the flight deck, artillery demonstrations, and sunsets on the open ocean—but for me, an undercurrent of easiness remained. Every time those fearful thoughts surfaced, I prayed. The Ready Room, with its comfortable chairs for briefings/meetings, offered a welcome refuge for Bible reading and journaling. I knew our confidants at home were praying for our sons' receptiveness when the time came for the anticipated family talk. Even in my uncertainty, the prayer covering was a great comfort.

In spite of these underlying emotions, I abandoned myself to total enjoyment of this great adventure. Without the use of cellphones and texting on the huge ship, I frequently had no contact with Steve and Mark. I was on my own for meals and activities unless I accidently ran into them in the labyrinth of corridors and stairs or in the Mess. Willing myself out of my normal introversion, I introduced myself and had many interesting conversations with other family members as well as Clark's fellow officers and superiors.

The caliber of the US Marine Corps officers/pilots was impressive. Graduates of the finest universities in the country, they were skilled professionals, well-spoken, extremely polite, and well-mannered. This select company made me even more proud of Clark's stature among them as a pilot and an officer.

The last day aboard ship, December 17, 2010, we awoke before dawn and gathered on the observation deck. It was a thrill to see land after six days of open ocean. What a beautiful sight it was to witness the sun rise from behind the California mountains. Heavy lift helicopters, one piloted by our son, were already on the flight deck with props spinning, preparing to take off, laden with Marine equipment and gear to offload to the Marine base on shore.

We civilians would debark later in the morning in large military landing craft standing alongside armored tanks, other vehicles, and heavy equipment being offloaded. We would then be transported to the "Welcome Home" hangar at Marine Corps Air Station Miramar, San Diego, in advance of the armada of Marine helicopters, crews, and passengers.

A large crowd waited several hours in the Miramar welcome hanger while the helicopters flew in and back out to the ship. As the final formation of aircraft circled the field and landed, the excitement of the crowd rose to a fever pitch. It was a grand procession as the men and women of the Marine Corps helicopter squadron left their aircraft, fell into formation, and marched toward the hangar to be joyously greeted by family and friends, most of whom they had not seen for seven months. Many young mothers with babes in arms were waiting to introduce their husbands to their new sons and daughters.

After that very long day, we left the base, rested a little at our hotel then found a nice restaurant for dinner. I prayed for a quiet place, but the restaurant was bustling with people all around us. We were seated at one of the few available tables in a semicircular booth. By the time we had finished our entrées, however, it seemed everyone else had gone. We had the place to ourselves.

We ordered dessert. *Lord*, I prayed silently, *give me the right words to say.* I was very anxious. Fearful thoughts had surfaced again. What would my precious sons think? What would they think about the half-brother they had known nothing about? I could only leave it in God's hands and hope and pray for their gracious acceptance. I took a deep breath, clutched my hands firmly together under the table and began to talk.

"Boys, we have had such a wonderful time together this past

week—a once-in-a-lifetime experience! I've been waiting until we were off the ship to tell you something that is very difficult for me to say, but at the same time, is really wonderful." I paused for a deep breath, glancing up at them with a forced smile.

"During my first year of graduate school, I was involved in a relationship and became pregnant. This was before I began dating your dad. The man I was dating arranged for an abortion, which was illegal at that time. The abortionist gave me an injection to induce labor and I passed a large blob of tissue. I thought that was the end of the pregnancy. I didn't realize until a few months later, it was not."

I paused, wondering how they were receiving my story, but could not look up at them.

"I went back twice and had one additional injection. After the third visit I had stomach flu symptoms and started hemorrhaging. My roommate took me to the student health clinic hospital, but I wasn't actually hemorrhaging—I was in labor and they referred us on to the Emergency Room. Soon after arriving at the hospital I delivered a two pound, ten ounce, live baby about three months premature. That was April, 1970."

I stopped again for breath. This time I looked up. They were listening, wide-eyed.

"The baby survived," I continued. "I signed papers to place him for adoption. All I knew was that after spending his first two months in the hospital and a month in foster care, he was adopted at three months old. It was a closed adoption—no contact, no information. In October, two months ago, a forty-year-old man contacted me in his search for his birth-mother. His description fit the birth circumstances exactly. I agreed to meet him with your dad. He and his wife came. He is a very fine man. He looks a lot like your grandfather Jones. His name is Michael Moore. He and his wife, Denise, have three children, eight-year-old twins, a boy and a girl, Evan and Emma, and a four-year-old boy, Aaron. We have met them all. They are very nice people."

"I went with your mother to meet them," Steve interjected. "I'm very impressed with this family and I really like the children."

"So what I am trying to tell you," I said carefully, "is that you have a half-brother you have never met. I never saw the need to tell you about my previous pregnancy because I didn't even know if he was alive; and besides, I was very ashamed about the whole situation. Now I'm grateful that it seems to have had a good outcome."

By this time I was crying and the boys were, too. Mark put his arm around me. "I love you, Mom. It's okay."

Clark agreed and hugged me, too. Then he looked straight into my eyes. "Mom, you've been thinking about this the whole time we were on the ship together, haven't you? And you didn't say anything?"

"Son, there are a couple of reasons. You had serious responsibilities on the ship and you didn't need to be distracted. Plus, it just wasn't the place to have a private conversation like this. Your dad and I agreed ahead of time we would have to wait until tonight."

They all slid in closer on the oval seat, their arms interlocked around me. They told me they loved me just the same as they always had. I felt very treasured and secure. They asked a few questions about Michael—where he lived and what he did for a living. However, this new knowledge was so difficult to grasp, they soon ran out of things to say. I told them I would like them to meet Michael, but it was up to them; no answer expected right away. They would need some time.

※

After two more days in San Diego, my husband and I left for home to get ready for Christmas while our sons stayed to move

Clark into his new apartment. We picked them up at the airport a few days later and went home to celebrate together.

On Christmas morning Michael texted me. "Merry Christmas! Would it be okay to call later?"

I texted back, "OK."

When he called, I asked our sons if they would like to talk to him. They said yes. Each had a short conversation with him. I was ecstatic when I heard one of them say, "We'll have to get together soon."

We did get together two days after Christmas at Michael's house where our sons met their half-brother and his family. We were surprised and pleased to meet Michael's parents, Connie and Jesse, as well. Michael requested a photo with him in the middle, his mother and father on one side and Steve and me on the other. It is a treasured picture and a tribute to his parents' grace, love, and openness to allow us to share their precious son.

Another treasured picture from that day is of my three sons— Michael with his two half-brothers on either side—a symbol of God's miraculous love and grace.

L to R: Steve and Bette Noble, Michael Moore, Connie and Jesse Moore.

L to R: Mark Noble, Michael Moore, and Clark Noble.

The children had a great time with all the guests, especially playing with Mark and Clark. On the way home Clark said, "They're good people. I'd like them even if they weren't relatives."

Ever since that first meeting, Mark and Clark have accepted Michael as a brother and his children as nephews and niece. It has been reciprocal as well. After meeting Mark and Clark, Emma saw her teacher in the grocery store, ran up to her and said, "Guess what I got for Christmas? Two new uncles!"

In the midst of these wonderful, positive connections, my elderly mother's response was very disappointing. She'd had no prior knowledge of the pregnancy. My parents were 700 miles away when I was in graduate school and I did not tell them anything. At my sons' insistence, I told her about Michael. Her response was that she wished she had not been told. She did not want to hear any more about it and did not want to meet him or his family, even though his children were her only great-grandchildren. It is my prayer that she will someday be able to accept them at some level while she still has the opportunity to enjoy them.

Unbeknownst to her, Michael and his family were among

the many guests she greeted at her 100th birthday reception. Due to her poor eyesight, they simply blended into the crowd and she did not know who they were. They were, however, able to meet my brother and his sons who had flown in from New York and California for the celebration. The cousins enjoyed meeting each other. My brother's oldest son, Hubbard IV, and Michael shared a conversation about music, composition, and guitars. Both are extremely talented musically. The younger sons, Ben and Brendan, just slightly older than Michael's twins, bonded together with their cousins and enjoyed a time of play. Unexpectedly, Evan and Emma, appeared in a family photograph with my mother when they decided to sit on the floor in front of the rest of the family group.

Gladys Jones 100th Birthday with her two children,
Jones/Noble grandchildren, and two of Moore great-grandchildren.
L to R Back Row: Clark, Steve, and Bette Noble, Hubbard M. Jones III
(my brother nicknamed Bardy), Hubbard M. Jones IV.
Seated: Mark Noble, Gladys Lacey Jones, Brendan and Ben Jones (Bardy's
younger sons) Front row on floor: Evan and Emma Moore (twins).

Bette with nephews and grandchildren
L to R: Ben and Brendan Jones, Bette Jones Noble,
Aaron, Emma, and Evan Moore.

L to R: Emma (9) and Evan Moore (9), Brendan (11)
and Ben (12) Jones.

First Cousins and Musicians
L to R: Michael Moore and Hubbard Jones IV.

Eleven

REDEMPTION

*A*long the journey to responsible adulthood and committed marriage, Steve and I had rededicated our lives to Christ at a worship service following a business conference. Encouraged by the speaker's admonition to find a church that preached the Word and salvation through repentance and faith in Jesus Christ, we began to attend such a church.

Both of us had grown up in Christian homes, attended church every Sunday, made professions of faith in Jesus Christ in our youth, and been baptized. However, during college and graduate school we had both left the church and attended only when visiting our parents.

Following our recommitment, we stayed with some friends on an overnight trip. That same night, they invited us to a prayer meeting with a house church group they were extremely excited about. Neither of us had been to anything like that before, but we agreed to go and were willing to participate.

At that house church, during the group prayer time, standing in a tight circle with arms around the person on either side, I prayed silently, *Dear Lord, thank you for bringing me back to You. I have been away so long. I have so many things for which to ask forgiveness. My immoral lifestyle in graduate school has been heavy on my heart. Lord, You know that I lived a chaste life even when I was almost engaged in college. After the breakup my senior year, it just seemed living a good life didn't matter anymore. Then came graduate school, the relationship with Alan, the pregnancy, the abortion attempts, and the pre-term baby placed for adoption. Please forgive me for all my mistakes. Cleanse my heart and bring me back to fellowship with You. Thank You for dying for me and taking my sin upon You.*

At that moment, as I repented and asked for forgiveness, I had a very real and powerful sensation of being enveloped and bathed in the warmth of the Holy Spirit. Praise God, He answered my prayer. I felt fully cleansed, forgiven, and redeemed. The date was April 19, 1980, *exactly ten years* to the day from Michael's birth.

For me, the prayer meeting experience was the beginning of the road back to a real relationship with Jesus Christ. Although there were other highlights along the way, perhaps the most significant spiritual milestone came after meeting Michael. It grew out of my decision to volunteer with a local ministry, Choices Pregnancy Care Center (CPCC).

In considering what I was being called to do in response to learning about Michael, volunteering time with the Care Center was a logical choice. Our church supported CPCC as part of its local mission outreach. After meeting with Ann, the director, to discuss opportunities, I volunteered to meet with the single mothers' "Encourage Me" group. They needed help in career direction and job searching, areas in which I was experienced.

It wasn't long before I realized God wanted me to work directly in crisis situations, to help support and affirm young women in crisis pregnancies, educating them on their options, and when appropriate, providing information on the positive aspects of adoption. This was a much more challenging volunteer function. Even though I had been a counselor in years past, I felt God calling me beyond my comfort zone.

Waiting outside the director's office at the Choices Pregnancy Care Center to discuss this more responsible function, I struggled with how much of my story she needed to know.

"Hi, Bette. Good to see you again." Ann greeted me warmly through her open door. "Come in and have a seat. I understand the single mothers' group has been encouraged and motivated by your visits to their meetings."

"Thank you. I've enjoyed being with them. I hope they will be able to use the information to find good jobs that suit their God-given gifts."

"That's certainly our wish as well. What brings you in today?" Ann asked. "If there are other services you can provide, we are certainly open to finding ways to use you here at the Care Center."

"I'm feeling I do need to provide some other types of service, but I need to tell you a little bit more about my story." I had the feeling Ann frequently heard confidential information from volunteers about their calling to help at the center.

"I would love to hear your story," she responded, settling back in her chair. "I thought there might be an underlying reason for your interest in our program."

"Ann, I have wondered frequently if my story would have turned out differently if there had been a pregnancy care center near the university when I became pregnant in 1969." I had blurted out my secret almost before I realized. "I went to an illegal abortionist trying to end the pregnancy, but his technique of giving an injection did not resolve the situation. I expelled something but remained pregnant until I went back for another treatment several months later. The doctor said I must have been pregnant with twins and only aborted one fetus. After the last visit I was rushed to the emergency room, and delivered a premature baby."

Ann leaned forward. "What happened then?"

"The baby boy survived and was placed for adoption. That was forty-one years ago. After a three-year search, Michael located me last year. He and his family have met my family and we have had a very enjoyable time getting to know one another. I feel now that I must meet directly with crisis pregnancy clients and talk about the benefits of adoption."

"That's quite a story, Bette. Our two children are adopted and I am not sure how I would respond if they searched for their birth parents. You say your son's family was open to this?"

"Yes, Michael's parents and his wife had been praying with him about his search. He had a strong desire to share Jesus with his birth-mother if she did not know him. He was pleased to find I was a Christian and working for a ministry."

"Wow! I've never heard of that as a reason for searching for birth parents. And believe me, I've heard many stories in my twenty-plus years with Choices." Ann looked thoughtful.

"But back to your request to meet with our clients, we would be glad to have you trained as a volunteer Client Advocate to be on the front lines with us, but because of the abortion attempt, even though it was not successful, there is a preliminary requirement." She looked directly into my eyes. "We must be sure you are spiritually grounded and secure in your forgiveness from your past before you go through our Client Advocate training and meet with our clients in crisis.

"We have found a wonderful resource, an eight-week group Bible study with a very effective leader. It is called *Forgiven and Set Free–A Post-Abortion Bible Study for Women*[7], by Linda Cochrane. This group study provides a spiritual underpinning that creates a sound foundation for post-abortive women to

---

7 Cochrane, Linda, *Forgiven and Set Free – A Post-Abortion Bible Study for Women*. Grand Rapids, MI: Baker Books, 1996.

minister to abortion-determined women. These are our most common and most vulnerable clients. The lives of their babies depend on Client Advocates who can provide a clear message of options with the love of Christ in their hearts and kindness in their words. You will need to successfully complete the study before becoming a Client Advocate."

"Ann, I know I have been forgiven for my past, but if that is your requirement, I will do it. I feel sure I need to be on the front lines helping women who are where I was forty-one years ago."

"Okay, I'm glad to hear that." Ann stood and gave me a hug. "We will let you know when the next study will start. Lynn, the leader, will be in touch with you. Thank you so much for sharing your story with me. I hope you will decide to share it with others."

As I walked out of the Care Center, I had no idea what God had in store for me in the Bible study.

A few weeks later, Lynn, the group leader for the Bible study, called me with the time and place for the group meetings. In our brief conversation, we found we'd known each other many years previously when she and her husband had owned a local business.

It was a small group of women who met on a Sunday afternoon at the Care Center for our first Bible study meeting. Lynn invited each of us, the three participants, to introduce ourselves and to tell why we had come to be in the study.

Christine was a professional in town and had had an abortion thirty years earlier. She had experienced a number of emotional issues over the years and had just completed a sobriety program. She had married the father of their aborted child. Her husband was also a professional. As a result of her abortion, her reproductive system was so damaged she was unable to sustain her pregnancies after marriage. Desperate to have children, they had adopted two infants who were now adults.

Lynn mentioned that in addition to our study, a companion course for men, *Healing a Father's Heart*[8], was also available. Christine was very interested and said she would talk to her husband about the two of them going through the men's study at home.

Susan was also a professional and had experienced two abortions as a young woman. Following her marriage she required surgery during her two pregnancies in order to close her cervix and avoid miscarriage. She was also placed on bed rest for six months to extend the pregnancies as long as possible. Even with these precautions the deliveries were early. Her children were now independent adults.

These testimonies further revealed to me God's grace in my life. My first pregnancy following marriage to Steve ended in the traumatic death of the fetus in utero at four months and required surgery to remove the remains. Until that time I had taken for granted the gift of fertility. Due to that early loss, the healthy pregnancies that gave us our two precious sons were appreciated at a much deeper level. Until the *Forgiven and Set Free* experience, I had not realized how much more praise was due to God for these subsequent uneventful pregnancies.

This powerful, intensely spiritual study was one of the most life-changing events I have ever experienced. I thank God for putting me in a position that required significant time in the Bible and weekly group discussion sessions. In our small group, we shared our common abortion experiences at a very intimate and deep level. Our leader had also experienced an abortion.

---

8 Cochrane, Linda, *Healing a Father's Heart*. Grand Rapids, MI: Baker Books, 1996.

During our discussions, she shared her personal history. Videos and readings provided valuable insights about abortion. We learned why forgiveness is so necessary for our spiritual and interpersonal health.

"For if you forgive other people when they sin against you, your heavenly Father will also forgive you. But if you do not forgive others their sins, your Father will not forgive your sins" (Matthew 6:14-15).

The most memorable extra resource in the study was a short film, "Tilly," based on a story by Frank Peretti. In the film a woman, married with three children, is taken into heaven to meet the daughter she aborted after the birth of her older children. The aborted baby was born alive but lived only a short time while she was held by a nurse. The nurse named the baby Tilly and arranged for her burial. In heaven, the mother spends time with her daughter on what would have been the girl's ninth birthday. Before returning to earth, the mother finally acknowledges Tilly as her daughter and hugs her.

The film made me realize how similar I was to that woman. I had never acknowledged the reality of the first expulsion as an abortion with the death of a baby, perhaps a twin girl, since boy/girl twins seem to run in my family. Since I remained pregnant after that first attempt, all the following years I had denied it was an abortion; just some bloody tissue.

The study caused me even more to celebrate Michael's existence. By God's intervention and miraculous grace, He had put Michael where his life would be saved. Despite his very poor prenatal environment and premature birth, God also preserved his mental faculties and mobility. I thanked God for giving me the tremendous blessing of hugging Michael on this side of heaven.

But what of the other twin, the other baby, the one who died in the first abortion attempt? Would I see her in heaven as the video depicted?

In II Samuel 12:23, David felt assurance he would see his child in heaven, the son who was born to Bathsheba but died as a result of sin:

"But now that he is dead, why should I go on fasting? Can I bring him back again? I will go to him, but he will not return to me."

By the end of the study, I was able, through God's grace, to not only forgive myself, but also to peel back those layers of long-buried memories and expose them to Christ's healing light.

Twelve

GO AND TELL

s the first anniversary of Michael's call approached, I began to look back on the wonderful events of the past eleven months. It was about that time that I began to hear a whisper in my heart of a new calling—a new directive from the Lord—and I was terrified.

A year before I had not known if the child I had placed for adoption was even alive, much less mentally and physically sound. I could not even imagine meeting him and never thought about hearing him sing or hugging his beautiful children—my grandchildren.

During the year after our reunion Michael had met Mark and Clark, his half-brothers who became instant uncles to Evan, Emma, and Aaron. My brother and his three sons met Michael at Mother's 100th birthday reception. He had sung and played guitar and piano with my oldest nephew, a gifted musician in his own right. My brother's younger sons had enjoyed their new-found cousins, Evan, Emma, and Aaron. We had attended a party to celebrate the birthdays of Clark, Aaron, and the twins in their common birthday month. Due to Connie's schedule conflict, I was invited to play the role of substitute grandmother at Emma's birthday treat (in lieu of a party)—a trip to a theatre production of *Beauty and the Beast* with a visit to the American

Girl doll store. My husband, Steve, had been invited to play granddad in place of Jesse at the boys' birthday treat—Monster Jam, a big truck event. We had attended the children's Christmas play at their church and enjoyed watching a peewee football game where Evan played and Emma cheered.

Lord, I prayed, *it's unbelievable to have been thrust into this new role with my newfound son and his wonderful family. What unexpected joy! Thank you, thank you!*

Sitting in my prayer chair early one morning in the midst of this reverie, I was trying to focus on my daily online devotion from *The Pocket Testament League.*[9] The topic was "Strict Obedience during your Days of Confusion," based on Acts 10:11-21.

The devotion described Peter's vision of unclean animals and the Spirit's instruction to eat them even though Jewish law said they were unclean. The Spirit also instructed Peter to go with a group of men, including one Roman soldier, sent by Cornelius. The commentary noted how easy it could have been for Peter to dismiss this vision as a bad dream or a temptation to be disobedient to Mosaic Law. An additional interpretation caught my attention:

> Remember the Spirit speaks like the wind—a whisper, a nudge—so it's not like Peter had a pillar of fire leading him through this experience. Yet Peter gained control over his fear and his doubts and chose to obey. This is a gigantic lesson for all of us and is one of the great keys to our Christian maturity—making the choice to obey despite our confusion, fear, or doubts.[10]

---

9 Day 126: Strict Obedience During Your Days of Confusion, The Pocket Testament League, www.ptl.org, September 26, 2011.
10 Ibid.

That's really an interesting perspective, I mused. *So perhaps Peter may have had fears and doubts, but chose to do what this strange dream told him to do. It might not have been as clear an instruction as we presume. If he had not been so committed to Christ, he could have put it all out of his mind and hidden or run out the back way when the men came. Peter was a human, just like us. Amazing!*

As I considered this insight about Peter, I realized that through the experience of becoming acquainted with Michael, the Lord had taken me on a yearlong journey of healing and redemption. At the beginning of the relationship, I had been terrified of being identified in Michael's church. Now, after the conversations with our pastors and with two other friends, all urging me to tell the story, and the *Forgiven and Set Free* Bible study, I felt the Holy Spirit calling me to speak openly about what He had done in Michael's life, my life, and with our family.

The first friend who had encouraged me to share my story was Stephi, who had been reunited with her birth granddaughter. The other friend, Kay, had prayed for me without knowing why during my first meeting with Michael. Soon after telling our sons, I summoned my courage and told her the full story.

Kay became quite emotional. "Bette that is the most wonderful story I have ever heard. I would give anything for the opportunity to have met my birth-mother and to have known my half-siblings." I knew she had been adopted, but did not know she had ever tried to contact her birth family.

"Unfortunately," she continued, "I learned my mother had passed away in her mid-thirties, long before I thought about trying to find her. The search information included her roommate's comments about her frequent reading of the Bible, which gave me hope that she was a Christian and I would see her in heaven.

"Oh, Bette," she continued, "you must come and share this with my ladies' Bible study. Your story tells how God heals and redeems. Maybe it will encourage someone else to connect with their birth family before it's too late."

Kay later attended my mother's 100th birthday party and enjoyed meeting my "new" son and his family. She acted as photographer for the event, taking many pictures of Michael and his wife and children and their interactions with the rest of my family.

Based on Kay's invitation, my plan was to slowly ease into the process of telling my story in a "safe" environment—in another town where I was unknown. She asked me to come in November, 2011, a little over a year after I had met Michael. But God had other plans. He wanted me to tell the story in public for the first time in home territory in a most challenging realm.

I am a very private person. No one except my husband Steve, Michael's birth-father Alan, my roommate Hannah who had driven me to the hospital, Vicki, the third roommate, and Margie, a later roommate and long-time friend, knew about the baby until I first shared the story with Matt, our retired minister friend.

In October, 2011, I was scheduled to give the devotion for the monthly elders' meeting (the Session) at our church. I had already prepared a short inspirational message.

During the September meeting, the elder who gave the devotion told a personal story about experiencing the hand of God while she was a medical missionary. As I listened, I felt an unmistakable instruction from the Holy Spirit, almost like a physical pat on the shoulder and whisper in my ear. *You are going to tell* your *story next month.* That would be the anniversary month of Michael's first contact.

God, you have got to be kidding! Not here. Not with this group.

Believe me, the Session was the last place I would have chosen. My thoughts went back to that morning's devotion about Peter. As if to insure my understanding that His whisper was really His instruction, God sent me another clear Biblical illustration.

The next day's devotion, entitled "Doing What's Difficult," continued with the next two verses, Acts 10:22-23a. Peter went downstairs, talked with the men, and invited them into the house. The commentary asked this question:

> Has God given you a mission you are reluctant to complete? What are you afraid of—ridicule, embarrassment, persecution? … What do you need to do today to complete what God has given you to do?[11]

I had committed to being obedient and these two devotions went straight to the heart of what God had challenged me to do. Although He was very clear He wanted this done, I needed some earthly permission as well. I took the next step and wrote a short version of the story, suitable for the elders' devotion, and met with Paul, the associate minister with whom I had shared the story early on. Paul was supportive, but not overly encouraging.

"I'm not sure that is the best place to tell your story," he said. "I think it needs a larger venue."

"I understand your caution," I said, "but it is really clear to me God wants this story told here in next month's meeting." He smiled, put his hand on my shoulder, and prayed for me.

My next step was meeting with the interim Senior Pastor, Dr. Jap Keith. I planned to read the script to him and ask for his approval to use it as my devotion for the Session. In my two years as an elder no one had presented such a personal and possibly controversial topic. As I neared the end of my text, I looked up and was amazed to see tears running down his cheeks.

When I finished, the pastor said, "My dear girl, did you

---

11 Day 127: Doing What's Difficult, The Pocket Testament League, www.ptl.org, September 27, 2011.

handle this by yourself all these years? That is pure Gospel! By no means am I going to block the Holy Spirit. I heartily approve of you sharing this with the Session. This is what we need to be doing all the time. It's the Gospel message of forgiveness and redemption. I'll bring the Kleenex!"

The evening of the meeting I was almost shaking from fear as the participants gathered. I prayed for calmness and control. Attendance that night was twice as many people as usual. Included were the Pastor Nominating Committee, of which my husband was a member, the newly-elected elders for the coming year, and all the staff. The Lord answered my prayer and calmed my spirit. He kept my voice unusually clear and my emotions in check so I was able to make it through the devotion. I concluded with a prayer at the end. After the meeting, almost everyone came by to give me a hug and thank me for sharing the story.

Later that night one of the members of the Pastor Nominating Committee emailed my husband and asked him to forward the message to me. She was a newly-elected elder and would not attend meetings again until the beginning of the next year. Her email said she did not approach me after the meeting because she was too emotional to talk. The message was too close to her heart. She had been adopted and lately had been considering trying to locate her birth-mother but was afraid of what she would find. I emailed her, saying the Holy Spirit might be prompting her and encouraging her to pray for guidance. I strongly urged her to move forward and try to make contact while there was opportunity.

On Sunday, I unexpectedly met her at church in a quiet place and asked if she had thought more about searching for her mother.

"Bette, I have thought about it a lot since your devotion. I'm just so afraid of rejection and what I might find out if she would agree to talk with me."

"I'll pray for you, Megan. I have a dear friend who did not

get to meet her birth-mother, but has had a wonderful connection with her half-siblings. Like you, she was frightened, but the results have been so positive. Continue to pray for the Lord's leading and for courage if you sense He wants you to pursue a search. As a birth-mother myself, I am so grateful for meeting my child on this side of heaven."

Since that first message to the elders, the Lord has opened more opportunities for me to tell Michael's story. The presentations have sometimes been made by myself, on other occasions together with Michael speaking and singing. For Mothers' Day 2013, Michael's mother Connie and I both spoke and Michael sang for the Sunday morning message entitled, "Two Mothers."

Encouraged by the response from that first public telling of the story, the Lord has given us numerous times to share this odyssey of being reunited with my firstborn son.

Sanctity of Life Sunday, January, 2013, Northlake Baptist Church
Speakers: Bette Noble and Michael Moore.
Musical Presentation: Michael Moore
L to R: Back row – Bette Noble, Michael and Denise Moore
Front row – Emma, Evan, and Aaron Moore.

Thirteen

THE POWER
OF PRAYER, LOVE,
AND FORGIVENESS

During our first meeting at the restaurant, Michael asked some questions for which I should have been prepared, but was caught completely by surprise.

"Ms. Bette, we've talked about a lot of things, but I have to ask before we go: Do you know anything about my birth-father? Is he still alive? Do you know where he is? And do you mind telling me his name?

"Michael, I have had no contact with him since the relationship was severed in 1970. I have no idea of his health or his location, but he may still be in the city where he moved after he graduated from the university. He was a graduate of the same university and you might find him in the online alumni directory where you found me. And certainly, I'll tell you his name. It is Alan Lankerson.[12]

"Would you mind if I try to contact him?"

"If you could wait a while I would greatly appreciate it. I am not comfortable about meeting him in person at this time. I am pleased to meet you and your wife, but this entire interaction

---

12 Alan Lankerson is an alias, not birth-father's real name.

is quite overwhelming to me right now. I understand you have great interest in meeting your birth-father, and I support your search for him. But please delay your contact at least until I can talk to my sons and have some time to process meeting you."

"Okay. I hope he is open to meeting me when the time is right. I guess I wasn't thinking about your situation and your family. I'm so excited to meet you, but for you, it's probably as much a shock as it is excitement."

"Yes, it is. But I am very glad you kept searching until you found me."

Michael did not mention his birth-father again for some time except for stating his desire to have contact before his birthday in April.

One morning in March, I opened my email and was shocked to see a picture of Alan (considerably more mature) attached to a Facebook message. I was not friends with him on Facebook, but he had used the messaging contact that does not require FB connection. I could hardly breathe as I read his message.

Subject: Hello from many years ago

Hello Bette,

It's been a long time…..I hope you and your family are doing well. From your internet profile and photo, it appears that you have had a great career and still look very much the same.

I'd certainly like to speak with you if and when convenient for you, or at least communicate via email. My address is Alan@—. Phone: ___-___-_____.

All the best, Alan

I called Michael in a panic. "Michael, have you made contact with your birth-father? He sent me a Facebook message with his picture early this morning."

"Mama B, I'm so sorry. I didn't think about him being able to get in touch with you. I called him last night and had a good conversation. He is open to getting together as soon as he can schedule the time. I'm excited he is willing to meet, but I'm so sorry he upset you."

Calmer now, I said, "It's okay. It was just such a shock to get that FB email out of the blue."

I felt I needed to respond to Alan and use the opportunity to say some things that had come to mind since meeting Michael. However, I was very wary about a continued email communication and did not want to establish an online "friendship." People I knew had innocently established online contact with former romantic interests, some of which had rekindled long dormant feelings and destroyed apparently solid marriages. My relationship with Alan had been intense and I did not want to risk going beyond basic communication about Michael. I prayed for guidance on what to say.

––––––––––

Hello Alan,

Yes, it has been a long time. I trust all is well with you. I feel I am in a very good place. I have been very blessed with a good marriage to a wonderful man, almost 40 years now, two fine sons, and a very satisfying career.

I am assuming that your email is related to a contact from Michael, the child who was born in spite of our plans in 1970. Michael had indicated that he would be trying to connect with you sometime soon. It is a tremendous miracle that he survived the pregnancy and premature birth with good health, high intelligence, and a great personality. Although it seemed like the most horrible thing that could have happened at the time, I am eternally grateful for God's grace that he is alive, was raised in a good home, is married to a fine woman, and has three wonderful children who are bright, personable, and handsome.

Even though I will not be in ongoing communication with you, I did want to take the opportunity of this Facebook messaging option to thank you, albeit belatedly, for your support back in that very difficult time and for your underwriting most of the financial obligation for the hospital expenses. The excellent extended care Michael received definitely saved his life and gave him a chance to be adopted. I realize in retrospect the enormity of your sacrifice to cover all of that. Although it is way overdue, I do sincerely ask your forgiveness for not appreciating all you did and also for any hurt I caused for not staying in the relationship. The doctor who delivered Michael and followed up with me afterward urged me to marry you and take the baby home, but I did not think at the time it was the right thing to do for us or for the child. With the perspective of 40 years and knowledge of the couple who desperately wanted a child, adopted Michael, and gave him such a superior upbringing, I still feel it was the best decision.

My personal Christian background had the most to do with the breakup. Although I obviously was not following my faith in any way at the time, there was still a part of me that connected with Jesus. I have since come back and have absolute confidence that all of my past has been forgiven and that the Lord has directed me to the relationship I have with my husband, the relationship we have with our sons, the church we belong to, the ministry I work for, as well as a 24/7 personal relationship with Jesus. That doesn't mean I am better than anyone else. I am still very human and have my many flaws, but my life has been redeemed, I have peace that I am on the right track, and help if I get off track. I have prayed for you and for guidance on how to respond to connecting with you. This has led to the decision to write instead of talk or meet. I respect your faith tradition and hope you may have sought a place of worship of your own.

My husband has known about the baby since before we were married. He went with me to meet Michael. Since then I have told the rest of my immediate family and our pastor.

I hope you get to meet Michael and his family. He is a very fine man, talented in many ways, and is married to an exceptionally talented woman. They are great parents and are raising some outstanding children.

It is very good to know you are well and I pray for your continued well-being. It was good of you to reach out at this time.

All the best to you, Bette

———————

Bette,

Thanks for your kind letter, and, of course, I have to honor your wishes not to establish any dialogue. Please know that I have no desire to disrupt your life any more than it has already been disrupted by the recent surprise, but I would have thought it would be appropriate to share thoughts about the situation. I'm not comfortable with this much private information flowing via Facebook email, so had hoped we could communicate via private email, but I'll take a chance and reply.

Before reverting to communication blackout, I would like to share a few of my own thoughts and a couple of ironies.

First, I had wondered often over the years if one of us would one day get this "knock on the door." If he had contacted me first, then I certainly would have tried to communicate with you discreetly to give you a heads-up; BUT, I realize how completely unique a situation this is and there is no roadmap for the best way to handle it, and, regardless, I am extremely pleased that he contacted me and I look forward to meeting him soon.

The call this week came as quite a shock, but I, too, had wondered if he had survived, if he were healthy, and had had a good life, so this does resolve that curiosity that I had felt over the years.

From my telephone conversations with Michael, I agree with what you wrote, that he has been blessed with great parents, and sounds like a very well-grounded guy. And smart, of course! I can tell that he has a strong religious foundation, which is good. The kids look very cute. I have been especially impressed with Michael's impeccable Southern manners. Obviously, his parents must be tremendous people to be understanding and supportive of his quest to learn more about his biological lineage.

I'll be glad to – and have begun to – provide him my family's health history—certainly important to an adoptee and his descendants.

Coincidentally, about three years ago, I tried to see if I could locate him myself. I searched a few adoptee search sites on the internet, as well as attempting to search by birth date for that hospital and city. But I was not successful and then discontinued the effort when I realized I would not know whether or how to proceed even if I did locate him. Apparently, from what he has said, that was around the same time he started searching for his biological family. He was very resourceful in finally locating you.

The second irony is that just a few months ago I thought about contacting you, had looked you up on the internet, and had drafted a letter, not with any purpose nor to open any dialogue, but just to ask how you were and to know you were doing OK. But I never acted on it. Incredibly, it was probably around the time that you and he met.

You did the right thing in ending the relationship. We were of different faiths, were in different places in our lives, different objectives, and the difficulty of the "Michael" event would have remained a cloud over us forever. Forty-one years ago is a long time. The pain I felt at that time healed many, many years ago and evolved into memories of good times and special friendship. Regarding my having paid the expenses, no thanks were due then or now. I did what was the right—and only— thing to do.

I also, had let my wife know 30 years ago about the situation just in case one day what did finally occur last week might eventually happen. Even though she and I are now divorced, we remain close friends, and I called her to let her know about Michael's contact.

I have not yet met Michael, although I would very much like to as soon as we can arrange it. From what I can tell from various photos, he certainly looks much more like you….coloring, features, etc. Hard to tell if he resembles me at all, but maybe I'll notice more when we meet.

I have had a good life thus far and look forward to the remainder. I am in great health again now, following a potentially life-threatening illness last year. Thanks to superior medical care plus the prayers of family and friends of all faiths, I am well and back to normal activities, including tennis.

Again, thanks for your letter. All the best to you and your family for continued good health and happiness—

Alan

———

As I reflected on this interchange, my heart was softened. I remembered after the first contact with Michael how desperately I needed to talk to someone who had a similar experience. I sensed Alan did not have a friend like my friend Stephi, who could provide guidance. I prayed again for Alan and felt led to engage in a dialogue for a limited period of time. The following exchanges ensued.

———

Alan,

Thank you for your kind letter in return. You are wise in your view of Facebook communication and after reflection, some additional communication may be in order via email. I have had more time to process than you and I become more comfortable as time goes on. So I am willing to open a limited dialogue.

Bette

———

Thanks, Bette.

There's a lot to sort through and digest, indeed. I noticed on Michael's Facebook "wall" that you had attended the kids' recent birthday party. Did it go well?

I hope to make time in the next couple of weeks to meet him. Any thoughts, suggestions, guidance would be appreciated since you have already been down this path.

Thanks.
Alan

Hello again, Alan.

Before responding to your question today, I would like to respond to some issues you raised in your return letter.

Regarding giving a "heads up," I would never have considered presuming on Michael's agenda and plan for contacting you, especially since having had no contact with you for forty years. I treasure that first phone call, as traumatic as it was. It was one of the most dramatic moments of my life and I am still amazed and very grateful he found me. I would not have stolen that moment from you for anything!

Regarding his looks, I, too, was surprised. I did not have the benefit of prior pictures; my first view was face-to-face when he greeted me and hugged me at the restaurant where we agreed to meet after two phone calls. I had envisioned a dark-haired man looking like you. I was shocked! He looked a lot like my father.

Thank you for the analysis of the relationship; that is an apt description, and it is comforting to have it come from you. The financial support was the right thing and much appreciated, but in today's culture, many young women are not so fortunate. I am, in retrospect, very grateful for your integrity and sacrifice in that area.

I am reminded of how overwhelming and somewhat threatening the first meeting was and how each new introduction to

Michael's world included an additional stretch and challenge. However, Michael and his family have been wonderfully open and receptive to me and my family and their common theme has been "thank you" for the gift of Michael to them. I know they will welcome you as well, his mother in particular. She says that Michael has been the joy of her life and she is so grateful for the opportunity to have him as their son.

I have discussed with Michael that all of this is new to me while he has been planning and anticipating a reunion for years. There is a presentation I have delivered that combines a business model from *Managing Transitions: Making the Most of Change*13 and the Exodus story in the Bible used as an example in the book. It seemed to help Michael understand that there was a lot more processing to be done on my end, as there will be with you. The premise is that the leader(s) of any initiative has already planned, processed, and discussed the changes before introducing it to those who will be involved in implementing the new organization, process, or procedure. The leader frequently forgets that those people need time to process and adjust in order to successfully operate in the new structure, as illustrated in the Biblical account of Moses versus the Israelites in the Wilderness. I think it is interesting that the time period with our situation and with Moses was the same. The good part is there is so much to celebrate on this end of the 40 years!

Bette

———————

———————

13 Bridges, William. *Managing Transitions: Making the Most of Change, 2nded.* Cambridge, MA: Da Capo Press, 2003.

————————

Thanks very much for all this. I'm very glad you decided to communicate. I appreciate it. It does help to be able to share some thoughts. It appears your family has really handled this so well, and that is a tribute to all of you. I'm not sure how many families could absorb this.

Another big question: how "public" is this for you at this point? Right now, I still see it as a pretty private matter. I asked Michael if the children view you as a family friend or relative, and he said they know you are a "new" grandmother, and that they also have a new grandfather whom they have not yet met. [Oh, that's me!!!] I have only told my ex-wife, my significant other, and an old friend who knew about the birth at the time. I do plan to confide in my nephew—now 45—who, as you may recall, was adopted at birth, as I think his perspective would be helpful to me.

Please do send me a copy of the presentation—sounds extremely relevant…..and I have sensed it already, i.e., Michael seemed ready to meet right away, and my head had not yet stopped spinning. But, I have decided to jump in, and I am meeting him and Denise for dinner Thursday.

Thanks again for letting us communicate.

Alan

————————

Alan,

Here is information on the presentation; but use it as you see fit for your own understanding. I'm excited you are getting together with Michael and Denise. You will be amazed at what a good experience it will be!

As far as how public this is, my husband has been very supportive and a good sounding board. He has also often answered, "I don't know. There is no guidebook to this situation!" I continue to be amazed and very grateful for the acceptance by our sons. My mother is the one push-back. I never told my parents. At the insistence of my sons, I told her about Michael. She is almost 100 years old and said she wished I had not told her.

Beyond the immediate family, I'm still mostly private. I have told a couple of people outside my family, including our pastor.

How the children view me—Emma introduces me as her biological grandmother, her father's birth-mother. Not sure if they know what that really means at age nine, but it won't be long before they do. And yes, it is an adjustment to be a grandmother, so welcome to the world of being a grandparent, quite a concept!

Bette

Bette,

We had a great evening….I was very happy to meet them. Now that I have seen him in person, I do see a real "composite."

Alan

Alan,

I am so glad you had a great first meeting. As Denise wrote to me not long after we met, "Enjoy getting to know your brand-new 40-year-old son!"

Having communicated with Alan through his first in-person connection with Michael in March of 2011, their reunion was a natural conclusion to the limited dialogue between us. Michael's birthday was the following month. I asked Michael and Denise if we could delay having a joint birth-parents' celebration for Michael's birthday until the following year. I am sure that was extremely disappointing to Michael. I apologized to him and to Denise for requesting separate celebrations. I sensed that he had envisioned having us all there to conclude his fortieth year of life and the year he met his biological families. I understood his desire, but I sensed a strong spiritual instruction—"No, not yet"—to meeting Alan in person.

Although Michael seemed to understand my reluctance to seeing his birth-father, he had no conception of the deeply conflicted emotions I felt. In fact, I had purposely not enrolled in the university online alumni directory, Facebook or LinkedIn until early 2010 because I did not want to be found by Alan or any of my old acquaintances. Other work-related needs had encouraged me in the previous year to drop my guard and connect with social media. Although the email dialogue with Alan was pleasant, I had no peace about being present with him for a joint event.

At the time, I was not sure of the underlying reason for this strong reservation, but during the *Forgiven and Set Free* post-abortion Bible study later that year I came to understand it. The Lord had done His part and saved and redeemed me, but there was more to be done on my part in order to let go of the past and receive the full measure of His forgiveness.

During the study, I came to realize the need for *me* to forgive. I was led through the process of forgiving those involved in my past, including Alan. But more importantly, I needed to forgive myself for my willing participation and the abandonment of my faith. The prayers I offered to God as I verbally forgave others and myself released me from the hold those memories still had on me. I was truly set *free*.

The following year as Michael's birthday neared, I was eager for my family to celebrate the event together with Alan, Erica[14], his significant other, and Michael, Denise, Evan, Emma, and Aaron. My stress level was extremely high in anticipation of the group dinner, but the meal time was an enjoyable celebration. The reunion with Alan and meeting his friend Erica went well.

———

April 19, 2012 (Michael's birthday)

Hi Alan,

It was a pleasure to have dinner with you and Erica and Michael's family to celebrate his 42th birthday. Thank you for a most pleasant reunion. I prayed for the time to be full of grace and positive interaction and it was indeed. It was so good to see your obvious affection for Michael, Denise, and the children. The Lord has blessed these new connections greatly. I enjoyed talking with Erica and am glad you have such a good relationship. Steve enjoyed talking with you also. It was a wonderful time!

Bette

———

Bette,

I/we enjoyed the evening very much as well. Good to have a chance to visit with both you and Steve. Over the years, I had

———

14 Erica is an alias, not her actual name.

always hoped we'd have a chance to visit again one day, but never dreamed it would be under these circumstances. What an amazing odyssey for all of us.

All the best, Alan

Michael's family and his parents have been incredibly gracious and accepting to both sets of "new" parents/grandparents as well as brothers, uncles, and cousins. Alan and his former wife had no children and his brother's only son had been adopted. Neither Mark nor Clark are married nor have children. Michael's children, the *only* birth grandchildren, are a special treasure to both our families.

Several events—Evan's football and baseball games with Emma's cheering, church and school Christmas pageants and plays, Aaron's kindergarten graduation, Emma and Aaron's piano recitals, and the twins' summer drama camp productions—have been enjoyed by as many as three sets of grandparents.

The mutual respect and openness shown by all parties have given us the opportunity to become acquainted with Michael's family. At the same time, we have made a conscious effort not to encroach on the established and most important relationships—the parents/grandparents who have been there since the beginning.

Connie and Jesse have made these interactions possible through confidence in their relationship with Michael and their faith in the Lord Jesus Christ. They have shown no fear of sharing their precious son with us. The common denominator has been the power of prayer, love, and forgiveness, guiding us through these unchartered waters of uncommon relationships.

Thanks be to God!

After the football game 2013
L to R: Evan, Aaron, Jesse and Connie Moore

After the football game 2013
L to R: Evan Moore, Bette Noble, and Michael Moore

Michael's forty-fourth birthday party 2014
L to R: Bette Noble, Evan, Michael, and Aaron Moore

Michael's forty-fourth birthday party 2014
L to R: Emma Moore, Steve Noble, and Evan Moore

Fourteen

PINK DOGWOODS

Where I live, the dogwood blooms are a sure sign of spring. Over the past forty-plus years, the white dogwoods have been a reminder of the final trip to the abortionist and the pink dogwoods a reminder of the birth. For many years, I played an internal mind game, trying to get past the actual day my first son was born without remembering. After returning to Christ and reaffirming my faith, that day became a reminder to pray for him, not knowing what his circumstances might be.

On that 2010 spring morning, the dogwoods were in bloom right on schedule. As I started to plan my day, I glanced at my calendar with a start, then looked again. Yes, it was April 19. It was the baby's birthday! I had almost passed it by as before. But this was not just any birthday. I remember lifting my hands and looking heavenward.

Dear Lord, has it really been forty years? How can that be? It seems impossible so many years have passed. Lord, I pray he is alive and well, in spite of his perilous beginning. It would be a miracle if he is still living. But Lord, you know. I don't know if I will ever have the opportunity to meet him, but maybe this fortieth birthday will prompt him to try to find his birth-mother. It's not up to me. The thought is frightening in many ways, but if he is alive, I hope someday to connect with him.

It was during the course of that fortieth year that Michael made contact with me by the phone call on October 11, 2010. A few months later, he made contact with his birth-father, Alan. That first year was momentous for us all. Three diverse families were brought together in ways we never anticipated. By the end of the year, my family was fully connected with Michael's and we were enjoying every get-together. In a similar manner, Alan's extended family had met and embraced Michael's family and celebrated a Passover dinner together.

As described in the previous chapter, the blending would take another year as the Lord worked in me to forgive myself and others in my past. In the process, He freed me from painful memories, from fear of new relationships, and enabled me to welcome and enjoy all of Michael's combined family gatherings.

Michael's forty-first birthday on April 19, 2011, was soon after his first contact with Alan. At my request, our families celebrated separately on that first birthday since meeting him.

For Michael's present, I wanted to give him something unique that would be a lasting symbol of the day of his birth. It had not taken long to think of the perfect gift. In the midst of the emotional upheaval connected with his birth, the pink dogwood blooms outside my hospital window were a source of beauty and comfort. My birthday gift to him was a live pink dogwood tree to plant in his yard. I included a card with a note explaining the significance of the pink dogwoods and the comfort their beauty had brought to that difficult time. The card also contained the legend of the dogwood blossom.

The Dogwood Blossom[15]

The blossoms are in the form of a cross—two long and two short petals. And in the center of the outer edge of each petal there are nail prints, brown with rust and stained with red, and in the center of the flower is a crown of thorns, and all who see it will remember.

The pink dogwood is said to represent the blushing of shame for shedding of innocent blood.

God has placed many reminders on earth that should cause us to glorify Him for His wonderful greatness, mercy, and love. Dogwood flowers can do just that.

Since that time, I have reflected frequently on the significance of the dogwoods in my memories of Michael's premature birth and his life, sensing something more I was to understand.

Lord, what is it You want me to know? Please give me insight into what the pink dogwoods symbolize beyond the beautiful but commonly-known legend. There must be something specifically connected with my relationship with Michael. Will You please reveal it to me? I feel it is important to the story You want me to tell. I await your answer.

Following a period of praying and researching dogwood husbandry, the Lord gave me understanding of pink dogwoods as a metaphor of what it means to be **adopted**, from both a **human** and a **spiritual** standpoint. Here is what the Lord brought to mind.

Pink dogwoods are typically not found in the wild. They are usually planted in special places and given the best of nutrients. Like pink dogwoods, adopted children are also placed in specially selected homes with good physical environments and good relationships between the prospective parents. God certainly

---

15 http://www.creationtips.com/dogwood.html

placed Michael in a wonderful home with godly Christian parents who were desperate for a child after numerous miscarriages. He thrived in a loving and nurturing atmosphere with a solid foundation based on faith in the Lord. Michael today is a strong Christian with a family of his own, is a respected professional in his field, and is a talented musician in his church.

From a spiritual perspective, we all are adopted by God through Jesus' sacrificial death for our sins. The Lord tells us in the words of Paul:

> "For those who are led by the Spirit of God are the children of God. The Spirit you received does not make you slaves, so that you live in fear again; rather, the Spirit you received brought about your adoption to sonship. And by him we cry, 'Abba, Father.' The Spirit himself testifies with our spirit that we are God's children. Now if we are children, then we are heirs—heirs of God and co-heirs with Christ, if indeed we share in his sufferings in order that we may also share in his glory" (Romans 8: 14-17).

As Christians, we are incredibly blessed that God saved us and redeemed us through the death and resurrection of His Son, Jesus. He provided the Holy Spirit to live in us and nurture us, the Bible to teach us and communicate His Word to us, and the Church where we can be supported, loved, and mentored by fellowship with other believers.

God has now transformed the pink dogwoods in my past from a reminder of a very difficult situation into a joyful symbol of redemption and adoption by the Lord, and of Michael's life with his adopted family.

The Lord has also given me a symbolic daily reminder of that transformation. For Christmas 2011, my pretty and talented nine-year-old granddaughter, Emma, unknowingly gave me a special gift of remembrance from her father's birth on that day back in April, 1970. She thought she was simply giving me her hand-drawn oil painting of my favorite flowers, pink dogwood blossoms. For me, it is a tangible symbol of all God has done through saving Michael's life and His power to transform ashes into such beauty. (Emma's hand drawn pink dogwood oil painting may be seen in color at www.unexpectedfamily.com .)

Two years later, Emma sent me another gift as a photo message on my phone. It was April, 2013, and she sent me a direct gift from the Lord, a picture of the first blooms on the pink dogwood tree I had given Michael for his birthday in 2011—a living symbol of Christ's redeeming love.

Emma's pink dogwood photograph

In the years since God connected us, Michael and his family have been such a blessing. I continually thank the Lord for this incredible gift of redemption and love—reunion with my entire "Unexpected Family."

Fifteen

EPILOGUE

M y prayer early in this journey of reuniting with Michael was for the faith and assurance that the Lord would lead me through whatever lay ahead, as my sons were told, and others were told as well. I prayed my sons would receive this revelation openly and process the knowledge about me in a way that would enable them to want to meet and greet their newly-found brother with love and acceptance. I also prayed He would redeem that dark time forty-plus years earlier, take away my fear, and enable me to speak openly about what God has done in Michael's life, my life, and in our family.

The family members have written their personal thoughts about this journey upon which we have all traveled.

IN THEIR OWN WORDS

Connie—Michael's adoptive mother:

"I am so glad Michael found his birth-mother and his birth-father. We have raised him always letting him know he was adopted, told him the story of when we came to see him, and that we chose him. He always has had a deep longing to connect with his birth parents and I am happy to share him with them. I am not threatened. I know he will always love me as his mother. I am just grateful in the midst of the circumstances of his birth the decision was made to place him for adoption."

Alan—Michael's birth-father:

"Michael's sudden contact in March 2011 brought closure to the unanswered questions I'd had for forty years. His addition, along with a daughter-in-law and three bright, enjoyable grandchildren, have given a new—and very welcome—dimension to my life. Since my ex-wife and I had no children, connecting with Michael and his family has been a special blessing.

"What is such an important part of this story is the incredible support and encouragement Michael's parents have given him. They not only supported his quest to locate and meet his biological mother and father, but they have also accepted us and made us all feel very welcome at family events.

"I realized from the beginning there were no guidelines and no 'roadmap' for how such a reunion might evolve, if at all. So I am very grateful for the relationship which has developed and continues to strengthen."

Mark Noble—Michael's half-brother (six years younger):

"When Mom first told us about Michael and how he contacted her, I was naturally surprised and a bit unsure how I felt about meeting him and his family. I told Mom I would like some time to think about it. I can be slightly shy meeting new people and a bit apprehensive approaching unfamiliar circumstances. My younger brother and I discussed meeting Michael. He was much more decisive and immediately said, 'Let's do it.' I agreed and was grateful to have his encouragement.

"Meeting Michael, his wife, and their three children for the first time was amazing. Michael is a great father and Christian leader of his family. Learning about Michael's journey growing up with his adoptive parents who set such wonderful examples for him and his sister was inspiring. His desire to contact his biological mother to ensure her salvation through Jesus Christ shows how he spreads the love of Christ to others. We all hit it off so well, I know that God has kept and guided this family under his watchful care.

"Since meeting the entire family, we have developed wonderful relationships. I love keeping up with the kids' adventures and progress. We have enjoyed a family beach vacation and I have begun to teach my older nephew how to surf. I am looking forward to the growth that God has in store for each of us as we continue to become closer as family. Case in point, as I chose groomsmen for my wedding in January, 2015, I chose Clark as my best man and my 'new' big brother, Michael, as a groomsman."

Clark Noble—Michael's half-brother (twelve years younger):
"Family is a word that carries immense meaning for me. I think everyone has a subconscious idea of what family is to them even if they have never defined it in words. Apart from my relationship to Christ, nothing comes before family since my family was and is close. When my mom initially told us about Michael, I think I had a natural tendency to protect that family intimacy. Consequently, I was resistant to the idea of Michael as a part of the family even though I didn't admit that to anyone or even to myself. Looking back, I thought it was fine if he met Mom and they talked, but be a part of the family?

"Mom planned for my brother and me to meet Michael and his wife and kids only a few days after she told us about him. As we drove to their house, I remember feeling somewhat anxious. I had a lot of questions going through my mind: What is he going to be like? What is his family like? And selfishly, what do they really want from us? I felt protective of my mom and dad in the event my new brother was not the type of man who could be trusted.

Once we arrived at their home, we shook hands, hugged and just sat down and talked. I think learning Michael had a strong Christian faith really helped me and made a huge difference in terms of my ability to understand why he had sought out my mom. Furthermore, realizing that he did not blame or feel any ill-will toward her blew me away. It was evident to me that he genuinely loved her for the very fact she was his birth-mother. Over time and more visits, I slowly began to embrace the idea of Michael as a part of the family and even as a brother. This was in spite of the fact he wasn't there on our family's annual Christmas trip, we didn't play or fight together as kids, and he had never attended one of the famous (to us) Noble Thanksgiving feasts.

"Meeting Michael and getting to know him and his family and accepting them as a part of ours has been a great thing. In light of the situation with my mom when she was a young woman, Michael has shown us all a model of grace. Additionally, seeing my mom face her fears and continue to go down the path of reconciliation and healing has been a huge inspiration to me.

"My dad has also shown what it means to be a Christian husband by being there for Mom and supporting her while being a strong protector and source of guidance through the whole process. What I initially resistated has now become for me a model of real grace and real family. All of this was only possible through God himself and I thank Him for taking a source of shame and fear and using His power to show us what His love in action really means. He has immense power to change lives and redeem the darkest situations through normal people who allow themselves to be used by Him."

Steve Noble—Bette's husband, Mark and Clark's father:

"It came as a belated surprise. Before our engagement in 1971, Bette informed me that she had given birth to a son in April, 1970. Bette's disclosure in no way changed my mind that we would be wed. Now, forty-four years later our relationship has matured and deepened in God's loving hands.

"After arriving home from her office one brisk October evening in 2010, Bette broke the news that she had received a call from and engaged in a brief conversation with her birth-son earlier in the day. She was bewildered about her next step. I cautioned her to be sure all his information checked out, which she did in her return call to Michael. I was quite proud of her, knowing the potential stress of such a call.

"Michael proposed that the two of them meet in the company of each spouse at a neutral site. Bette and I discussed his proposal and agreed to meet at a mutually suitable location. We were in prayer for this meeting every day following Michael's first contact.

"It was a joyous reunion for both Michael and Bette. Denise, Michael's wife and mother of their three children, and I retired to a more remote table while Michael and Bette talked and shared photos.

"Within the following month, Bette and I were introduced to their children and later met Michael's parents, Jesse and Connie Moore. For them Michael was the answer to many years of prayer. When they were approached with the opportunity to adopt a child, Jesse and Connie agreed to visit the baby who was to become their son. God's hand played no small role in their acceptance of a tiny, underdeveloped three-month old infant.

It became known to us that Connie had had numerous miscarriages and they had given up having a child of their own. Jesse and Connie trusted in the Lord's leading and raised a son who has pleased them and his Savior. A grateful and humble man, Michael is a leader in his home, church, and community."

Michael:

"Mama B, I am so glad to know you and your family. I have always wanted you (and my birth-father) to know I was alive and how God has greatly blessed me in my adopted family. Even before I knew about some of the circumstances, I knew I needed to be prepared to understand what you had been going through when I was born and you placed me for adoption. I knew you needed to know how good God had been, how he'd kept me alive despite being a preemie. I wanted you to see what God had done. I am so glad that together we are now able to tell our story of God's great blessing to help bring about healing in the lives of others."

Bette—Michael's birth-mother:

"Through the redeeming love of Jesus Christ, He has answered all my prayers and more—far more—than I could have ever imagined or dreamed. Michael is alive and whole. He is a successful husband, father, and professional in his field as well as a lay minister and musician. His children bring great joy to their 'new' grandmother. My family has not only accepted him and his family, they have embraced them. Fear has been overcome. I have proclaimed—and will continue to proclaim—God's wondrous ways and blessings imparted to our new-and-expanded-'Unexpected Family.'

"Thank you, Lord. Praise be to your Name."

Crown Global Reunion 2013—Celebration Banquet
August 3, 2013, Stone Mountain, Georgia
Testimonial—Bette Noble, Musical Presentation—Michael Moore
Back row: Michael and Denise Moore, Bette Noble,
Chuck Bentley (CEO-Crown Financial Ministries), Steve Noble
Front row: Aaron, Evan, and Emma Moore

POSTSCRIPT

*T*he four years since Mark and Clark were introduced to their previously unknown half-brother have been a wonderful time for us all. Mark's marriage to Linda Sigle in January, 2015, is a shining example of the beautiful relationships formed and the universal love and affection evident, as well as the loving reception by our extended family to the "new" relatives.

I was excited to know the Moores would be among the family members, including siblings, cousins, and their spouses— all gathered for such a special time in Mark's life. But I was even more delighted to learn Michael and his children would take part in the wedding. I could hardly believe it when we all arrived at the wedding location, united in such a way only God could have orchestrated. Mark's beaming smile was contagious and I found myself smiling throughout the ceremony and reception.

In a way it was a fairy tale wedding for me, the mother of the groom and the mother of three such fine sons. What a joy it was to be escorted down the aisle by both Clark and Michael—Mark's instruction as revealed to me at the rehearsal. How exciting to see Michael's children honored by their roles in the ceremony. Emma gave the Scripture reading on love from I Corinthians. Evan, a junior usher, helped to roll out the runner for the center aisle, and after the ceremony, escorted me to the reception. Aaron served as the ring bearer. All three children performed exceptionally well.

The entire wedding weekend demonstrated to me the remarkable depth and width of the Lord's redemption and the great beauty created from the ashes of that time long ago.

Thank you, Lord.

Three Brothers Ready for the Wedding
L to R: Clark Noble (Best Man), Mark Noble (Groom),
and Michael Moore (Groomsman)

Mother of the Groom, Bette Noble, escorted by sons,
Michael Moore and Clark Noble

Aaron Moore, ring bearer,
nephew of the groom

Dr. and Mrs. Mark and Linda Noble

Noble and Moore Families
Back row, L to R: Clark Noble, Denise and Michael Moore
Front row, L to R: Emma Moore, Bette Noble, Mark Noble, Linda Sigle
Noble, Steve Noble, Aaron and Evan Moore

*Now to him who is able to do immeasurably more
than all we ask or imagine, according to his power
that is at work within us, to him be glory in the church
and in Christ Jesus throughout all generations,
for ever and ever! Amen.*

(Ephesians 3:20-21)

ELIZABETH (BETTE) NOBLE

 **Bette Noble** is a native of Florida, born in Ft. Myers and reared in Miami. She graduated from Stetson University with a major in mathematics and minor in psychology. She was a doctoral student at the University of Georgia, earned a Masters in Science degree in Applied Psychology with additional doctoral coursework. She taught statistics and psychology at the college level and worked as a behavior specialist and program director for state mental health and retardation programs. She was assistant director for children and adult mental health outpatient and residential programs in a large regional program area.

For many years she served as a research and development coordinator for career, personality, and financial assessments and a technical writer of business and economic updates for Crown Financial Ministries. She continues with Crown as an assessment and research consultant. She is also an independent career management and job search consultant.

Bette now concentrates on speaking and writing on pro-life and adoption topics based on her experience as a birth-mother and birth-grandmother. She and her husband have served their church as both deacons and elders. Her husband, Steve, was recently elected to serve on the Pastor Nominating Committee for their church. They live in Northeast Georgia and have two adult sons and one daughter-in-law.

Unexpected Family is Bette's first non-technical publication.

Credit: Author image by http://www.lifetouch.com

CPSIA information can be obtained
at www.ICGtesting.com
Printed in the USA
LVHW042007140420
653421LV00012B/1339

9 780578 159256